Body Language Basics

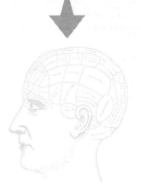

SHELLY HAGEN

BORDERS.

Published by
Adams Media,
an F+W Publications Company
57 Littlefield Street, Avon, MA 02322. U.S.A.
www.adamsmedia.com

ISBN 13: 978-1-59337-569-0
ISBN 10: 1-59337-569-7

Printed in Canada.

J I H G F E D C

This publication is designed to provide accurate and authoritative information with regard to the subject matter covered. It is sold with the
understanding that the publisher is not engaged in rendering legal,
accounting, or other professional advice. If legal advice or other expert
assistance is required, the services of a competent professional person
should be sought.
—From a *Declaration of Principles* jointly adopted by a
Committee of the American Bar Association and a
Committee of Publishers and Associations

Many of the designations used by manufacturers and sellers to distin-
guish their products are claimed as trademarks. Where those designations appear in this book and Adams Media was aware of a trademark
claim, the designations have been printed in initial capital letters.

Interior illustrations ©1990 Studio Editions.

*For bulk sales, contact your local Borders store and ask to speak
to the Corporate Sales Representative.*

contents

1 WORK THAT BODY! • 1

2 FIRST IMPRESSIONS—
AND PERCEPTIONS • 15

3 NOT-SO-PRIVATE EYES • 33

4 FACING BODY LANGUAGE • 47

5 GRAND GESTURES • 63

6 TAKE A STANCE—
CAREFULLY • 80

7 MAKING CONTACT • 94

8 AROUND THE WORLD! • 108

9 THE DATING GAME • 123

10 LIAR, LIAR • 140

INDEX • 154

iii

CHAPTER ONE: Body language: What is it, what's it for, how can you spot it in others, and what can you do to make it work for you? Maybe you feel like body language is kind of a silly pseudostudy. If we all use it, it's just what humans do—so we must understand it already, right? Probably not as well as you'd think. Knowing the facts about body language gives us the skinny on what's really going on at work, at home, or at this week's book club meeting (are these ladies really happy, or are those constant smiles fake?), and knowing how to control our own bodies can make our communications that much more effective.

THE HISTORY BEHIND THE STUDY

Researchers in incredibly varied fields have been interested in humans' capacity for nonverbal communication for thousands of years. In fact, rumor has it that the ancient Romans were even interested in tying the spoken word to the body's movements.

Body language falls under the studies of:

→ Anthropology

→ Biology

→ Neuroscience

→ Evolution

→ Linguistics

→ Sociology

. . . and under the category this book will put it into, which is everyday, got-to-know-this-information. (No term paper due on this, but you will take a quiz or two!)

Charles Darwin, who gave us the theory of evolution, is credited with really advancing the study of body language in the late nineteenth century. After noting that humans and animals had similar means of expressing emotions through facial movements, he formed a theory: It was necessary to understand how animals expressed themselves emotionally before we could truly understand how humans express themselves, as all of this is linked by evolution. Since animals obviously let their bodies do their talking, Darwin theorized that humans followed suit.

In the 1970s, an anthropologist named Ray Birdwhistell developed the theory of kinesics, which is the study of body movement. He based much of his work on Darwin's theories, and is considered an expert in the field of body language.

Most researchers in this field theorize that all of us have three "sets" of body language:

1. Natural or inborn body language, like when you turn red when you're angry.

2. Learned body language, like the "We're number one" hand signal.

3. Signals that are a mix of the two. These vary from person to person, but crying is one example. We're all born with the ability to cry; some of us learn to "use" it for personal gain or for attention in certain situations.

Fact is, every single person gives off hundreds of non-verbal messages every day—and we respond to hundreds more. There are varying estimates as to how much of our daily communicating is accomplished through body language (some range as high as 90 percent), with most estimated percentages settling right around the 75 percent mark.

"What?!" you ask. "How can I be sending signals that I'm not intending to send?"

Very easily. Read on.

COMMUNICATION AT ODDS

Often, we know exactly which signals we're sending. We're angry with someone, we confront them with our hands on our hips, eyebrows down, and a low, assertive tone of voice. This follows Darwin's theory, by the way, that everything about us—including our body language—has evolved from the animal kingdom. While animals don't strike a stance with paws on hips, they will attempt to make themselves seem larger in a confrontation (which is what the hands-on-hips stance is all about), and they will adapt their facial expressions and "voice" patterns to aggression. Watch an animal get angry sometime (and keep out of his way). You'll note that humans use some of the same tools to express themselves in times of conflict.

Though there are some similarities in the types of body language humans and animals employ, there are also some major differences in how some of those signals are interpreted. This is why body language plays a major role in training a dog, for example, as there are certain movements that show the dog that the trainer is dominant. Dogs naturally respond to these signals.

Talk, Talk, Talk

Of course, humans also have the gift of language, which only complicates matters. You see a dog getting angry, and you know what he's thinking. He's not pretending to be angry in order to manipulate a situation. With a human . . . you can't always be so sure. Anger, happiness, sadness—any emotion can be faked through body language. Moreover, we sometimes unintentionally say one thing while our bodies act as a billboard for a completely different message.

What happens when humans' words start contradicting their body language? We tend to believe the body language in these cases. Imagine this: You're having a romantic dinner with a charming man, and he's telling you how interesting you are. He just can't get over your beauty, your intelligence, and your incredible sense of humor. And yet . . . as he's talking, he's looking over your shoulder, he's watching the waiters walk past your table, and he's fiddling with his silverware.

Later, you're wondering what the heck that was all about. He told you all the right things, and yet . . . you were left feeling that something isn't quite right. It's because his body language was telling you a completely different story, which happened to send you the exact opposite message: He's not interested. (We'll get into the specifics of the signals he's sending off here, and we'll cover more romantic crises in Chapter Nine.)

When someone tells us one thing with their mouth and something different with their movements and expressions, we tend to believe the physical expressions, even if we don't realize it. It's because of this lack of realization of the disconnect between the spoken word and body language among humans everywhere that we often find ourselves confused about what's really happening in our relationships.

The man in question is obviously unaware of the contradiction between his spoken message and his movements. After all, he's indicating through his body language that the words coming out of his mouth are untrue. (Why he's contradicting himself, we may never know, but if he were aware of the signals he's putting out, you can be sure he'd change either his verbal message or his nonverbal one.) If you can learn to read body language, you can walk away from a situation like this with a fairly good idea of where you stand with someone, no matter what you've been told. (More on personal relationships in the next section.)

The Art of Body Language

After reading this situation, you may be thinking, "Ah-ha! Now I can deconstruct all of those quirky personality types I'm dealing with!" Maybe with a little learning and a lot of practice you can, but it's not always as easy as knowing which signals are sending which messages. There's a bit more involved in reading others' nonverbal communication.

Although Darwin's theory tells us that we're born giving off certain signals, these signals aren't always involuntary. In other words, even though body language is an innate trait, it can also be learned—and manipulated. This can be a good thing, as in the case of acing a job interview by using your posture effectively, or it can be a bad thing, if a used car salesman convinces you with his eyes that the hunk of junk on the showroom floor is actually primo transportation.

Body language is also specific from person to person. As in the case of the seemingly disinterested date, his body language might be telling you that he's just a highly distractible person. It's not really fair to judge a person in this situation based on one interaction. What's more important in personal relationships is to look for patterns of behavior and disruptions in those patterns (some mothers can tell, for example, when their kids are lying to them simply based on the child's body language—the stance, the eye movements, the telling shoulder shrug, all of which differ from the kid's normal behavior).

Learning the Ropes

So why should we learn to read body language? We can really only use it when we're face-to-face with someone, which means that when we're thinking someone on the phone is lying to us, we'll still be in the dark. Well, there's lesson number one: It's easier for someone to lie to you over the phone, precisely because it's easier to tell a whopper when you're not worried about your body language giving you away. If you know, for example, that you tend to purse your lips when you're being less than honest, and you're telling an untruth face-to-face, you may try to control this movement—which may exacerbate the situation and, in turn, your body language, giving yourself away all the more. Tell the same lie on the phone, your tone of voice may well conceal your true intentions, and your lips can tighten up as much as they want—they'll tell no tales other than the ones you intend to tell. Literally hiding our body language is a great relief in certain situations—but knowing which movements give our true message away is important, in any case.

Understanding body language can enhance our personal, work, and social relationships. Knowing how and why others send nonverbal messages essentially opens up a whole new world of comprehending people, their personalities, and their motives.

Consider how learning about body language could help you in this situation: At the office holiday party, you spot the coworker you've been dreaming about for months. She's coming your way, and you're getting sweaty. You want her to know that you find her attractive. She stops to speak to you, and you're suddenly rocking back and forth on your feet, jingling the change in your pocket, and looking down at her feet. She walks away, unsure if you're having a seizure and wondering if she should call a paramedic. You think you've blown it for sure. Your body language told this woman that you're extremely nervous in her presence—and what she does with that information now is out of your hands. (Will she steer clear of you, or will she read your signals correctly and find your nervousness endearing? Either way, your intended message—that you like her and that you'd like to know her better—got lost during your little jingling dance.)

How could this have gone differently? If you can learn to control—manipulate—certain aspects of your body language that you find undesirable or that are simply not working for you in specific situations, you'll walk away from similar interactions feeling as though you sent the right message (instead of a quirky one).

Wow. Pretty confusing stuff. Must be time for a test.

DECODING THE MESSAGES

Before you get into the rest of this book, test what you already know about how others present themselves without saying a word. How can you tell, for example, if that guy at work really digs you? How will you know if your neighbor has truly led the most amazing life or is just a fibber? And what kinds of things do you need to watch for in your own body language, so that you aren't divulging information you'd rather keep to yourself?

Number Two Pencil, Please

You really could use a Number Three pencil, or a pen—or a crayon, for that matter. Jot your answers down; the answers and their explanations are contained in the following section.

1. Your boss walks into a meeting and shakes the hand of the division manager. You notice that your boss offers his hand with his palm facing the floor. Any special significance to this gesture?

2. Why do politicians love to use those rehearsed hand gestures? Don't they know how phony they look?

3. When you put your feet up on your desk and yawn while talking to a subordinate, what kind of message is this sending? Are you tired, lazy, or simply relaxed?

4. You're on a date with a woman who is smiling, smiling, smiling at everything you say. In fact, she hasn't stopped smiling yet. Is this girl for real?

5. Lifting the eyebrows when you're talking to someone: sign of dominance or interest?

6. You're leaving a meeting with a colleague, who puts her hand on your back as the two of you walk out the door. Should you be concerned?

7. Your brother's Adam's apple is constantly jumping up and down whenever you talk to him. Does this indicate that he's being less than truthful?

8. While speaking with your neighbor about her reign as the Queen of Sheba, she constantly touches her face. What should this tell you?

9. A coworker insists on crossing her arms every time you speak with her. Why is she on the defensive all the time?

10. What does your mascara say about you?

11. Although he assures you it's all right that you lost an important file, you can see your boss's neck turning red. Is he just anxious, or should you start looking for a new job?

12. Your teenager is lying to you for the umpteenth time this week—you think. This time, she's raising her eyebrows to drive her point home. Believe her or not?

13. A date refuses to look you in the eye. What's that all about?

14. Your best friend has this way of telling a story with her hands flapping in front of her, palms facing upward. Why is she doing this?

15. While arguing with your loved one, you're disturbed to see him draw a completely blank face. What's he saying by doing this?

The Answers to Life's Questions

All right, there may be a few questions about life that aren't answered by this book, but these are still important facts. Here we go with the explanations:

1. Your boss's palm-down handshake is a gesture of dominance. In other words, he wants to make it very clear to the manager that this office is run by him (meaning your boss). More on the handshake in Chapter Two.

2. Politicians find themselves in a tough spot: Hiding the hands is a sure sign of dishonesty (but there are many,

many hand signals that indicate dishonesty, as well). Most people assume that politicians are not 100 percent honest, however, so most choose a set of hand gestures that show the hands behaving in a fairly consistent manner whenever they speak in public. The movements are rehearsed, but more importantly, they're controlled.

3. This set of signals indicates that you are comfortable in your position and that you're not going anywhere—i.e., the subordinate should just keep on working around you and your throne.

4. A smile that goes on and on and on is probably not genuine. Look at her eyes. If you can see that her crow's feet are fully engaged, the smile is more likely to be real. More on facial expressions in Chapter Four.

5. Lifting the eyebrows while you're speaking to someone can have several different meanings. This gesture essentially underlines what's already written on your face. In this case, as long as the rest of your facial features are registering interest, it shows in your raised eyebrows.

6. Shuffling someone out the door in this manner is a show of dominance, and may mean that your colleague views you as less than her equal.

7. An Adam's apple is not susceptible to emotion; if your brother's Adam's apple can't sit still, it's a physical thing, and not an indication of deception. If he's constantly clearing his throat, however, he may be lying. The throat tends to close up when one is nervous or uncomfortable.

8. Touching oneself on the face, neck, arms, or wherever may be a sign of a dishonest person trying to pull the wool over your eyes. But this is a case where you need to know more about this person to establish a pattern. She could just be nervous about something unrelated (though her recent dethroning is likely the cause).

9. Contrary to popular belief, the arm cross isn't a surefire sign of being on the defensive. Sometimes, it's just a comfortable position. Look at how the arms are crossed: Are they pulled into her body tightly? She may be nervous. Are the arms loose and out to her sides? She could be pulling the classic increase-her-size maneuver, which is a sign of dominance.

10. Makeup is an interesting little topic. Women's attempt to widen their eyes, conceal their less-than flawless skin, and plump up those lips is an attempt to appear younger, and the theories explaining the reason behind this are similar: The first is that we're just trying to attract men, who are inherently drawn to fertile, young women. The second states that we're actually trying to echo a baby's face—which makes men feel protective of us.

11. Flushing of the ears, neck, or face is often the first sign (and, in cases like this, sometimes the only sign) of impending anger or rage. Flushing can also occur as a result of anxiety, so it's important to assess the situation and other body language cues. (For example, if your boss also won't look you in the eye, you've got a big problem. Go home and look through the want ads.)

12. As mentioned before, the eyebrows are there to drive home a point. When someone raises their eyebrows while speaking, it's often an indication that they believe the words that are coming out of their own mouth (and hence are telling the truth as far as they know). Take that for what it's worth when a crafty teen is involved.

13. Refusing to look a new mate in the eye isn't necessarily a sign of disinterest or deception. In fact, the gaze-down, as it's called, can be read as a sign of submission, and is quite common in new relationships. Also, eye contact differs among cultures, so if your date is Japanese, he's probably just being polite. More on eye contact in Chapter Three.

14. Palms-up is generally a sign of goodwill towards humanity. Your friend is trying to draw people to her by using this hand motion. In a business setting, the palms-up gesture is often an attempt to build a bridge.

15. The blank face is the ultimate statement. It says, "I'm not here. Go away." Actually, all of us use the blank face in social situations all the time—when we walk through the grocery store, for example, we aren't all smiles and raised eyebrows. Even if we make eye contact with someone, we're likely to look away quickly.

So . . . how'd you do? The important thing to acknowledge is that body language is real, and it's all around us, all the time. It affects all of our communications, as much as or more so (in some cases) than the spoken word.

first impressions— and perceptions

CHAPTER TWO: Body language plays a crucial part in sending first impressions, which is why it's so important to be aware of the signals you're sending, especially in a business setting, where these initial nonverbal signals can be the difference between success and doom. We all know people who are so charming, so enchanting that they can lead an hour-long meeting about nothing, and we come away feeling as though we've really benefited from the experience. Body language has a lot to do with that. This chapter will discuss body language in the workplace—and how to make it work for you.

THE HANDSHAKE

The handshake is really an art form. You get it right, you're golden (or at least you've made a good impression). The handshake says a lot about how you view yourself, whether you're confident or meek, whether you're caring or disinterested. Make sure you're sending the right signals when you shake.

Shake It Like You Mean It

A good handshake includes the following characteristics:

Clean, well-manicured, dry hands and palms. The appearance of your hands shows you care about the image you're sending forth—it's also indicative of your lifestyle. (Men with soft hands are living the high life, it's assumed.)

Pleasant smile or an open face and level eye contact. This welcomes the other person into your little world.

Extended arm and hand. Gestures of friendliness—you're literally reaching out to the other person.

No invasion of personal space. Keep a comfortable—but not ridiculous—distance between the two of you.

Hand vertical—palm not facing the floor or the ceiling. The palm-down move says you're the stronger person. Vertical palm indicates you're on equal footing.

Firm grip—but not so firm as to cause pain. A good grasp in the shake shows your confidence. Be careful not to give the bone-crushing shake, though, as this is a sign of dominance.

Palm-to-palm contact for at least three seconds.
Again, you're sincerely welcoming this person into your world or you're accepting the invitation into theirs.

Now, the proper amount of up-and-down shaking varies from region to region. In New York and Boston, for example, colleagues tend to shake three to five times in quick succession. In Los Angeles, however, you tend to get only one or two shakes. Keeping the shake going longer than that sends off awkward vibes—as though you're holding hands instead of just greeting one another.

Adding one simple move to the handshake indicates your perception of your confidence and character. Note how big-wigs routinely grab the other person's elbow or cover the other person's hand during the shake. You shouldn't try this while shaking with your boss, but when dealing with subordinates, it sends a signal that you're in charge, but that you're also concerned for them. (And you are, aren't you?)

Remember: Your handshake speaks volumes about who you are and what you're prepared for. You have three seconds to make that impression. Make sure you're doing it right.

The Dead Fish

Say no more, right? We've all experienced bad handshakes. It's a pity, really, when bad shakers don't correct themselves, because the characteristics of a weak handshake are easily remedied—recognizing that a problem area (or two) exists is the most difficult part of this whole exercise.

The effects of a bad handshake are long-lasting. Try to remember a time when you came in contact with a bad shaker. What kind of message did it send to you about the other person? Did you want to shake that person's hand again? Did you go out of your way not to? What kind of effect might that have had on your business relationship?

These may seem like silly questions, but remember: Most of our communication is nonverbal, and a situation like this, where we avoid or dread a handshake, can have a domino effect. The other person sees our eyes darting about the room, doing anything we can to avoid shaking hands, and before you know it, we have a communication crisis on our hands.

Of course, this book is not suggesting that you go ahead and correct a coworker's bad handshake. Just be aware that there are certain characteristics of a bad shake; try to avoid making the following errors when shaking hands:

Sweaty palms. Indicates nervousness and/or less-than-honest intentions. If you can't stop the sweating, do anything you can think of to dry your palms before you shake. Wipe them on your pants under the table if you must.

Limp grasp. Suggests timidity or nervousness. Grab that other hand firmly.

Not enough palm contact. Don't be afraid of hurting the other person's hand—get those palms together. Offering only your fingers suggests that you are under the delusion that you are royalty—or that you're a scaredy cat.

Palm facing the floor or the ceiling. The palm-down gesture suggests domination. The palms-up gesture actually indicates that you're an open, honest person, but it's just not the standard for a handshake, and may leave the other person feeling confused about the position of your hand and what the heck you're doing. Save this nonverbal trick for when you're speaking.

If you suspect that you're a bad shaker, practice on someone who'll be brutally honest with you. You really can correct this before your next big meeting—and there's no time like the present to get your handshake solidified.

BODY TYPES

Judge not, we say, and yet we do it all the time without even realizing it. Society values and devalues people based on appearance—whether it's the relative attractiveness or the size and shape of a person. How and why does this happen, and who does it more—men or women? More importantly, how does this affect our body language, and how can we use body language to overcome negative judgments from people we don't even know?

Weight of the World

The harsh truth is that society tends to judge overweight people as being lazy, unintelligent, and incapable of a high level of work. After all, the thinking goes, if your obese coworker were in control of her life, she'd be thin; if she can't control her weight, then how well can she handle her work? We tend to view fit coworkers in the exact opposite way, as being younger than they actually are, bright, popular, and productive. Fit people also tend to intimidate those of us who aren't in great shape, because we feel they have "one-up" on us.

There are exceptions to this, of course. Not everyone falls prey to this type of thinking—but most of us do it without even realizing it. This is one huge way that body language shapes our society.

We start judging people based on their body types when we're children: Unattractive and/or overweight kids are judged by their peers and teachers to be lazy, dumb, sometimes jovial, and yet ultimately unpopular, while good-looking, normal-sized kids get better grades and are more successful in their peer relationships. If we're making these kinds of assumptions in childhood, it stands to reason that they would carry over to our adult interactions. And if we're the ones who have always been overweight, always accepting the negative judgments, our body language will communicate how we feel about ourselves.

So the mission here is twofold:

1. We need to recognize our tendencies to judge others—negatively and positively—based on their body type.

2. We need to recognize how we respond to society's judgments of our own body type.

This isn't a psychology book, and I wouldn't presume to get too deeply into how negative body stereotyping can affect someone's self-esteem, and how that can affect every aspect of his or her life. Just remember that you do have control over the way you carry yourself and how you present yourself to others.

Judgment by Gender

In general, women tend to be more judgmental of body types and features than men—at least when they're judging other women and themselves. Women tend to diet more than men do, so they tend to notice when someone else has lost or gained weight. They're also quicker to notice and point out other "adjustments," as well—like when someone's had plastic surgery.

The reason for this is simple: Women are encouraged from the time they're small to be pretty and attractive, which in our society equates to being thin. Anything else they can accomplish after that is like icing on the cake. Pretty girls get the best dates. Pretty women marry the wealthiest men. Pretty women are favored by the boss—and by society in general. It makes perfect sense that women are more sensitive to appearances.

Men, on the other hand, tend to be judged (and to judge fellow men) on how much power they have, physically or financially. (This also supports Darwin's theory of evolution, where the strongest survive.) Men tend to be most concerned about others' appearances mainly in social settings—which is why the prettiest girls get all the dates.

Is it fair that we're judged by something that's largely out of our control? Of course not; it's just the way life is. Again, we have to realize that we have control over the messages we send through our body language. We may not all look or feel like supermodels, but we can certainly express our level of confidence through our physical movements—or at the very least, we can learn to fake it.

IMAGE IS EVERYTHING

After reading that last section, you may be thinking, "What? Why should I fake anything? I like who I am!" Fair enough. Chances are, you already have an air of confidence about you and don't need help making a good first impression.

For those of us who tend to make a bad first impression, though—or worse, no impression at all—it's time to re-evaluate what's happening with our nonverbal communication and to change what isn't working, especially if you seem to be running into major roadblocks at work. If you've been consistent in your productivity and yet the rather incompetent schmoozer down the hall got that big promotion over you, maybe it's time to look at the way you're presenting yourself. It may have more of an effect than you think.

Walking Tall

First impressions often begin with someone's posture. Consider the message you want to send to coworkers or employees: Do you want to appear in control, or do you want to seem scared of a challenge?

Standing (and sitting) up straight with your chest out is a power posture. It tells others that you have confidence in yourself and that you aren't afraid of people or difficult situations. Walking with your shoulders back tends to give you a nice gait, a definite stride (but not a strut), which further enhances your image. You appear young, healthy, and vibrant, ready to take on the world—at least in the corporate quarter. So, walk tall, and swing those arms naturally with your palms facing the rear.

Slouching, conversely, tells the world that you have no faith in yourself or your abilities. Walking slumped over sends the message that you have no vim, no vigor, no get-up-and-go. Maybe you appear ill, or maybe you appear tired, and maybe you garner some sympathy from this posture—but you're not winning any votes of confidence. People who slouch also tend to shuffle their feet along which only strengthens the unspoken message that you just don't have the energy to deal with anyone or anything.

Slouching can also lead to physical discomfort in the form of backaches and headaches. If you tend to slouch, make a concerted effort for just one day to straighten up. Have someone take digital pictures of your normal posture and your new and improved posture. The difference between the two will be obvious at first glance—perhaps even surprisingly so.

In addition to walking like you have a broomstick taped to your spine, you should also take note to walk with proper speed: Too fast, and you'll look like a chicken with its head cut off (which makes you look not only a bit goofy, but also nervous); too slow, and you'll look like you're ready for a vacation (or that you're already on one). It's best to adopt a tempo that's somewhere in the middle—brisk, but not exactly fast.

Eye Contact

You've heard it a million times: Look someone in the eye while you're speaking to them. But for how long? When should you look away?

Staring at people while they talk to you is not good eye contact. It tends to make the other person nervous, and it can also be taken as a gesture of dominance, as when the conversation is of a fairly serious matter and you just refuse to look away. It's like a game of chicken to see who'll back down first.

Making too little eye contact is not conducive to a productive conversation or meeting. Depending on mitigating circumstances (and your body language), a lack of eye contact can indicate apathy, disrespect, and/or a lack of comprehension. Try to maintain eye contact for about three seconds. Any longer than that, and you're risking coming across as hostile or dominant; any less, and you may appear nervous or deceptive. Look off to the side when you break the gaze (more on this in the section on interviewing later in this chapter).

Something to throw in with the initial eye contact: a little raise of the eyebrows. This maneuver shows your interest in the other person, showcases your open (and welcoming) face, and draws the other person's eyes to your own. You've just showed this other person that you're not the least bit hostile towards them.

Of course, there are the eye moves that really have no place in a business meeting, among them eye rolls and winks. We'll discuss these and more information about what your eyes are telling other people about you in Chapter Three.

Palms-Up

We've already covered this briefly, but we'll mention it again here: The palms-up gesture, especially in a business setting, indicates an intention to close a gap or to build a bridge between two sides. It's meant as a friendly, open motion, drawing you in to the speaker's point of view. It should be interpreted as a non-hostile invitation to join whomever is speaking in whatever it is he's proposing.

Drummer Boy (or Girl)

Feeling nervous? Bored? Just plain musical? Best to keep this out of the boardroom by not drumming your fingers, pens, or pencils on the table. This will be interpreted as rudeness by your coworkers, and really shows a lack of interest on your part.

Same goes for your feet. Even though in many cases, they're hidden behind a desk or under a table at work, a habit of jiggling or tapping those feet can show in your upper body (coworkers will wonder why your top half is bouncing in a rather strange manner while you're seated). Save that tappin' for home, where you can really cut loose.

Grooming

It sounds obvious, and yet there are so many people who neglect to take care of their outer appearance.

We just discussed how people are sometimes unfairly judged by things that are out of their control—how attractive they are, or how thin or fat they are. When you look across your cubicle wall and see Marie, the woman who apparently hasn't combed her hair in a year or more, you're bound to make some sort of mental note about her lack of concern about her appearance and what it says about her. Is she so lazy or unconcerned about her appearance that she can't spruce herself up a bit? Has she fallen on hard times and can't afford to take care of herself? Does she just not realize how bad she looks? If that's the case, why is she being trusted with sensitive information? Whatever the root cause of Marie's hair problem (no pun intended), her lack of grooming translates into a lack of professionalism.

Image doesn't begin and end with hair, obviously. Take special care to make sure your hair is neatly combed, and then make sure your clothes are relatively in style (they don't have to be fresh off the runway, but current with the era); that your stockings are free of runs (ladies only); that your hands are clean and moisturized, and your nails are trimmed; and—every bit as importantly—make sure that your shoes and accessories are in good repair.

You can get away with a less-than-perfect appearance when you're just out of college. You get to a certain age, though (late twenties, early thirties), when you'll start to notice that the people getting promotions are the ones who are well groomed. Yes, this sounds like advice from a 1950s-era hygiene class movie, but it's the truth. The way you take care of yourself tells everyone around you three things:

1. Your level of professionalism.

2. Your level of intelligence (because you know you have to look good at work).

3. Your intentions for the future (because you know that well-groomed folks get ahead faster).

You'll feel more confident, which will show in your body language, which will only benefit you in the long run.

ACING THE INTERVIEW

So here's the scoop on interviewing successfully, and you've already guessed it by now: Your body language is going to do a lot of the talking. It's up to you to make sure it's telling your potential boss (or her director of human resources) the right things.

You've read about the handshake, eye contact, and personal space—all of these carry over into the interview. For kicks, let's look at a mock interview situation. See if you can spot any potential trouble spots in this scenario.

Robin Reports for the Interview

Robin is interviewing for a spot with a *Fortune* 500 company. She dresses in her black pantsuit, whips her hair into a neat twist, and carries her briefcase along with her. She walks into the office with a steady, straight gait—shoulders back, head level.

Her interviewer, Ms. Smith, invites her into the office where the interview will take place. They shake hands in the doorway, Robin gives her the eyebrow raise, and Ms. Smith places her hand on Robin's back as she enters the office. Robin takes a seat, cross-legged, with her briefcase on her lap. She sits up straight, maintains constant eye contact with the rather relaxed Ms. Smith, and answers all questions with brief, to-the-point answers. She seems well qualified, which is fine and well, but many of the other applicants will have similar credentials. So . . . where does Robin stand after the interview?

Robin, Relax!

Robin's experience and appearance definitely work in her favor. While she can't fake the right answers, she has presented herself pretty well, at least in her outer appearance. Whether she's a natural beauty or not, she chose an appropriate outfit and hairstyle for the interview (she's obviously done her research and learned that big corporations expect their employees to dress conservatively). We'll assume that the rest of her appearance is as well cared for: her nails, her shoes, her handbag, and briefcase.

Note how Robin took great care to maintain her power posture while entering the office, and that she was careful to give Ms. Smith the eyebrow raise. Note, too, that Ms. Smith took the opportunity to show Robin who's in charge here by walking her into the office with a hand on her back.

Could Robin have improved her interviewing body language skills? Yes. She sat with her legs crossed and with a briefcase on her lap—drawing a definite line in the sand between her and Ms. Smith. A more relaxed, open position would have included Robin with her feet flat on the floor (or crossed at the ankles) and with her briefcase on the floor next to her chair. She would have looked at ease, but not inappropriately so.

Her eye contact was also a problem area. Constant eye contact comes across as being dominant or just creepy. Robin would have been wise to break away every few seconds by naturally looking off to either side and then returning to Ms. Smith.

Take special care to look to the side of the person you're speaking to—never down at the floor. Breaking off your eye contact into a downward gaze can be interpreted as an act of submission, or even as an attempt to be deceitful—which are not the ideal signals to send during an interview.

Another trouble spot: Sitting ramrod straight during the entire interview isn't likely to score Robin any big points. Yes, yes, it's important to have good posture and to avoid slouching—but in an interview, it's also important to assess and reflect the interviewer's body language—and to do it without the interviewer knowing it. In this case, we know that Ms. Smith is a relaxed kind of gal. Let's say she leaned forward onto her desk to ask Robin a pointed question or two. Robin would have done well to answer those questions by also leaning forward—just a bit. Ms. Smith might use a lot of hand gestures when she speaks. Robin might have also thrown in a slight palms-up gesture of her own once or twice.

Lastly, Robin was quiet during the interview except to briefly answer Ms. Smith's questions. To show that she was completely engaged in whatever Ms. Smith was saying, Robin might have tried nodding and/or slightly tilting her head and responding to some of her points with a simple, "Um-hmm," from time to time. This would have shown that she was listening and truly thinking about what Ms. Smith was saying.

Summing It Up

Reading about Robin's interviewing experience is fine and well, but how does this translate into your successful interview? Read the following summary of good interviewing body language:

Proper attire. You'll look good, you'll feel confident, and that will come through in your body language, just as sure as wearing the wrong clothes will make you feel uncertain about yourself. Big companies expect conservative clothing; creative industries are more lax.

Good posture. Walk into that office with your shoulders back and your head held high. You look confident and ready for a challenge.

The shake. Just right—firm, not too long, no sweaty palms.

The face. Open. Inviting. Eyebrows up initially. Smile when greeting your interviewer, and then maintain a somewhat interested look by nodding from time to time, taking care to smile when it's appropriate.

Eye contact. Not too much, not too little, no looking down at the floor.

Feet flat on the floor. No bags in your lap; no crossed arms. These are barriers between you and your interviewer.

No tapping those feet or fingers. This only shows your nervousness. Also, keep those hands still for most of the interview—no playing with your buttons, your fingernails, or anything else. This shows that you're nervous.

Hand signals. If you're a big hand-talker, try to keep it under control in the interview. Palms-up gestures are fine when used in moderation.

Lean forward. Show the interviewer you're really interested in what she's saying, especially if she's leaning forward, too.

So much to learn! Do people really study and use these interviewing tricks? You'd better believe they do—and some of those people are your competition. Body language is powerful, it's real, and it does determine in many cases who gets the job. Know how to use it to your advantage.

Reading Between the Lines

All right, so now we know where Robin could have improved her interview scores—but what about the strange things that interviewers do when they're evaluating you? Knowing how to read the person who's firing questions towards you is sometimes as important as projecting the right image of yourself—you'll know what this person is thinking, and whether there's anything you can do to correct the situation.

The handshake. You know the drill. It's all dominance.

Eye contact. If your interviewer is not making eye contact with you at all, assume he or she is disinterested and don't count on getting this job.

Rearranging papers, winding the clock, straightening pens, etc. Ditto. For some reason, this person has no interest in what you have to say. The position may have been filled already, or your skills may not match up to the job.

Leaning forward. Your interviewer is really interested in what you're saying. Make sure to match her body language by also subtly leaning forward at some point—without making it obvious.

A radical change in position. If your interviewer was leaning forward, seemingly hanging on your every word, and has suddenly reverted to a rigid upright position in her chair, you may have said something that she has either found troubling or that took her by surprise. This may not necessarily be a bad thing, but she may need time to assess the new twist you've added to the interview.

Fingers in the steeple position. Brace yourself. Something big is coming. This is the classic position an interviewer takes when she needs to break something to you gently or when she needs to ask a particularly probing question.

The best way to ace an interview is to practice, practice, practice. Knowing the right things to say is part of the battle—knowing how to emphasize your point through body language can swing the vote in your favor.

not-so-private eyes

CHAPTER THREE: How many times have you found yourself telling a story to someone, only to realize that your listener is staring off into space? Something tells you that this person is not truly engaged in what you're saying—but how can you tell for sure? And what about that guy in your apartment building who winks at you every time the two of you cross paths? Is he just friendly, or would he like to become more than friends? The eyes may be the windows to the soul, but you may feel as though those windows need a good cleaning so that you can see the real message behind them. This chapter will let you know what those eyes are up to.

KEEP IT ON THE LEVEL

When your boss walks into your office to let you have it for something you've done (strictly a hypothetical situation, of course), does he pull up a chair and get right down to discuss matters with you, or does he stand above you, glaring down into your face? Whichever tack he takes says a lot about the kind of communicator he is.

Now think about your own life: The last time you confronted someone, or the last time you simply had a one-on-one, heart-to-heart conversation, where were you in relation to the other person? You may not realize that your position says as much as the way you're using your eyes to convey certain messages (which we will certainly discuss in more detail later in this chapter).

The View from Up Here

When you stand above someone, you're literally looking down on them as you speak—and it's coming across that way in the figurative sense. Being on this higher physical plane as you make eye contact with someone is a sign of dominance—whether you mean it to be or not. Really, it's not so hard to imagine this being true; it happens in real-life situations all the time: A parent regularly stands head and shoulders above a child while admonishing him or her. Someone giving a presentation is standing, while everyone else is seated, looking up from the conference table. Teachers walk up and down the aisles of a classroom, peering down at their students as they speak. What do you notice in each of these scenarios? There's little equality between the speaker and whomever is being spoken to. Carrying this technique over into interpersonal relationships sends the same message: One person has more power than the other.

Imagine this: You come in the door from work, ready to settle the argument that began between you and your significant other earlier in the day. He's seated on the couch, looking up at you. You proceed to initiate the conversation, never sitting down. While he may hold his own in the conversation verbally, chances are you're going to feel dominant as you're looking down at him. When you feel dominant, you're more likely to act dominant. The repercussions of doing so in this situation may be positive or negative, but the point is . . . they may come about because of how you're using your dominant eye contact, and not because of any brilliant points you're making with your speech.

The person whose eyes are at the highest level in a conversation or a business setting is sending out the signal that he or she is the person in authority.

This is not to say that it's a bad thing to use the higher eye level in your daily life. It's simply important to understand its meaning and to interpret its effects correctly. (You may try to use the same argument on your loved one during an eye-level conversation a month later, to no avail. You'll know why.)

Even Steven

Now picture the same situation—but this time, you've seated yourself on the couch next to your guy. You've just evened out the playing field a bit. You're looking at one another on an equal level, which may help to promote a more equitable level of conversation. Where you were more likely to dominate the conversation in the previous example, you're more likely to use some give-and-take tactics here, allowing your mate equal time in the conversation.

When a parent really wants to get a point across to an errant child, the wisest thing that she can do is to get down to the child's eye level. Looking the kid directly in the eye—instead of glaring down from a bird's-eye view—engages the child in a way that using pure dominance can't.

When a parent peers down on a child from high above, the child feels nothing but fear (much like a husband might feel while he's seated on the couch and his wife is staring down at him). Engaging the kid in eye-level conversation to rectify a wrongdoing is much more effective in the long-term, as he's more likely to listen to what you say to him.

Now, how about that boss? What's the appropriate response when he enters your office and starts browbeating you from on high? That depends on how gutsy you are, and how willing you are to engage in an actual confrontation. If you want to make this conversation less of an attack on yourself, slowly (slowly—a too-quick motion here will only signal hostility) rise from your seated position so that the two of you are conversing on the same physical level. He may be able to throw every complaint in the book at you, but he'll probably feel less dominant (if only a smidge less so) if he's not looking down at you. Suddenly, you've become another adult and less defenseless-seeming. If you're planning on pleading your case, doing so at eye level will be far more effective than defending yourself from your seat.

Now, if you're truly scared of the guy, or you think he's a goofball, or you have no intention of uttering a word in your own defense, you can use your eyes to convey these very messages. We'll discuss how to talk with your eyes in the following section.

WE HAVE CONTACT!

Eye contact is a tricky little thing to get a handle on, whether you're trying to decipher someone else's use of it or whether you're the one trying to use eye contact to your advantage. Often, it comes down to the simple question of how much eye contact is appropriate, and how much is just too much?

As with all body language, the answers depend on the situation. The amount and type of eye contact that's appropriate in a well-seasoned (and comfortable) relationship is not the same eye contact that one should use on a first date. Likewise, the eye contact you use in your personal relationships is different from the eye contact you use in the boardroom. This section will delve into the amount and types of eye contact in order to give you a good overview of what your gaze is saying to those around you.

Glares and Stares

We've all done it: Used a hard glare on someone we aren't at all happy with. Why do we do this? Well, because it's meant to intimidate the other person, of course. So what's the difference between this use of the eyes and the lingering gaze across a crowded room? In both instances, we're looking at another person for longer than is socially acceptable, conveying a nonverbal message through the length of the eye contact. But in the first case, we're pushing the other person out of our intimate circle, and in the latter case, we're trying to draw them in. How the heck does the other person know which message we're sending?

Easy. Body language seldom exists in a bubble (something you'll realize as you read through this book—interpreting someone's entire body language communiqué is always the safest route to uncovering their true message), unless the person practicing it is a master of controlling his or her unspoken communication (which you will be when you complete your reading). In other words, eye contact is usually accompanied by other telling body signals.

When someone is glaring at us, for example, his eyes may actually be bulging, his eyebrows may be furrowed, his jaw may be set, and his stance may be intimidating (all concepts we'll discuss later in this book). These are definite signs of anger and hostility. On the other hand, when someone is staring at us in an inviting way, his face will be more welcoming: A smile is an obvious sign of friendliness, as is an eyebrow raise (which is often used, along with a thrust of the chin, in lieu of a spoken greeting between coworkers or acquaintances).

The eye contact in both situations is enough to tell us something is up—and yet, the messages are completely different. Most of us will have no problem deciphering the positive message from the negative one—but the next time you find yourself returning a stare or a glare, take note of the rest of the body language signals that are completing the message. This is a study in human nature, and a sure signal that we are still hanging onto our primal methods of communication.

Winks

All right, so there's usually an obvious difference between a glare and a stare. What else do the eyes have to say?

Picture this: You're at a meeting in your office, seated across from a coworker you've always found rather attractive. The two of you have worked closely on the project being discussed and have recently buried some bad news about it. When your boss mentions how well the project is progressing, you lock eyes with your coworker, who winks at you.

What the heck was that all about? Is it the suit you're wearing? Is it the way you've fastened your rather tight bun this morning? What is it about you that he finds so irresistible today, when he's never seemed to notice that you're a member of the opposite sex?

Well, hate to break it to you, but he may still be a lost cause. A wink generally means that people involved are sharing some sort of secret—the definition of which can vary greatly, depending on the person doing the winking. In this case, it's obvious that the coworker is sending a signal that says, "If they only knew what we've been through to put this project together!" But a wink can also say, "I find you attractive—just between you and me." Someone who winks all the time is eager to appear as a confidant—their winks say, "You can trust me. We have this secret bond going on."

In general, winks of the sort described here often mean less than we interpret (or want) them to mean. They're usually used with the intent to convey a cute little message— that you and the winker actually do share some sort of secret, or that he may find you attractive. The problem with a wink is that it's so ingrained in society as a sign of intimacy that very few people actually use it for this. As a result, it's often used in a cutesy, jesting, or overtly flirtatious manner, though we still tend to want to find deeper meaning in it because we think we know that it's a visceral, involuntary action. (This guy is so swept off his feet by our beauty that he can't control his eyelid!)

The wink can really be classified as one of the learned body language signals that we discussed in Chapter One. Bottom line: We need to let go of this as a sign of a truly significant, love-laced message.

Blinks

Your supervisor blinks nonstop—or maybe it's your sister, or your neighbor. Whoever it is, the blinking drives you up the wall. What's up with that, you wonder? Is it just a matter of dry eyes? Might this person benefit from a vial of eye drops?

Perhaps. There's no denying that some people blink a lot because they simply have some sort of eye discomfort going on. However, blinking can also be a sure sign of stress or excitement. The next time you notice someone blinking like a string of Christmas tree lights gone haywire, take note of the conversation and/or situation. Is there anything about it that might be causing this person some kind of distress—or something that might be giving this person a thrill?

Blinks are common as a courting ritual ("batting" the eyes), when we're faced with speaking to strangers, and when we're lying. Under these circumstances of elevated anxiety levels, the brain releases a surge of the chemical dopamine, which, among other physical effects, can cause our eyes to go a little overboard with the blinking.

So . . . can we learn to control this behavior? Of course. This isn't as difficult as, say, regulating our heartbeat (something completely unseen that also happens in situations where we're more tense than usual), but it requires concentration. After all, how much thought do you really give to your blinking? But what's the point? Why should we bother trying to control it if it's something we never give any thought to in the first place? For the same reason that your supervisor's (or sister's, or neighbor's) blinking drives you mad—because it sends a signal to whomever you're speaking to that there's a hidden message behind those flickering eyes.

Whatcha Lookin' At?

What's more aggravating than trying to talk to someone who refuses to look you in the eye? Precious little, really. We expect that when we talk to someone, they will meet our gaze—not to do so indicates a lack of interest in what we're saying . . . or does it?

Yes . . . and no. It's disturbing to converse with someone who won't divert their eye contact (in other words, every time we look at them, their eyes are fixed on ours). As we discussed earlier, this can be interpreted as a sign of aggression. If the conversation has a friendly overtone, you can probably bet that this person has probably tried to figure out the language of eye contact—and failed. Meanwhile, if your listener is constantly staring off to the side of your head, you may wonder if his eyes are simply misaligned (he's almost looking at you . . . but he keeps missing your eyes) or if he's just too nervous about something concerning the conversation to look you square in the eye.

Stop yourself there. Before you accuse this person of having less-than-honorable intentions because he can't seem to look you in the eye, take note of the different ways people break their gaze during normal conversations:

The initial contact. People greet one another and hold each other's eye contact for only a matter of seconds before looking elsewhere. The length of time for the initial eye contact varies depending on how intense or close the relationship is.

Looking down. After the initial eye contact, we tend to look away. Looking at the floor (what's referred to as the "gaze-down") indicates that we feel submissive to the other person—or that we aren't being truthful.

Side to side. The best way to naturally break eye contact without sending any hidden messages is to look off to the side of the speaker and then re-establish eye contact throughout the conversation. There are some theories as to whether it's best to look to the speaker's left or right, but for our purposes (which include maintaining a positive relationship and not appearing bored or disinterested), it's safe to say that using either side as a focal point is all right.

Look up, look down, look all around. Actually, don't. Looking at everything going on around you and the person you're supposedly engaged in conversation with sends the signal that you could not possibly be less interested in this interaction. You may actually be able to observe the world around you while simultaneously focusing on what the speaker is saying, but it won't appear that way to someone who doesn't know you well (or even to someone who does).

Aversion techniques. It's an old trick that mothers around the world use—forcing children to make eye contact as a means of determining whether the kids are being truthful. It works. Inexperienced liars break eye contact before they can get the fib past their lips. Averting your eyes goes hand-in-hand with looking everywhere but at your conversational partner, except instead of sending the message that you're completely disinterested, you're showing that you have something to hide.

No one's home. When we close our eyes during a conversation, what kind of message does that send? It says to the person we're speaking with, "I don't want to hear this. I'm not here. I'm not engaging in this dialogue." We send a similar message if we fail to make eye contact with the other person, opting to adopt a blank stare. We're telling this person, "I'm not even paying attention to you. I'm here, but I'm not here." Both of these moves are interpreted as being disrespectful, so don't go using them as a way to simply escape a conversation. There will be consequences.

Remember, these examples apply to deciphering Americans' use of eye contact. The significance of eye contact varies widely from culture to culture. If you're planning a trip overseas, it's in your best interest to bone up on what's appropriate body language and what's not. We'll discuss some of these concepts in Chapter Eight.

If you know that your own method of making and maintaining eye contact could use a little work, then by all means, work on it! Rein in your eyeballs; stop avoiding other peoples' eye contact; use the side-to-side technique during conversations. Knowing how to use these skills to your advantage is as important as learning the right things to say. You might just see an immediate improvement in your interpersonal relationships.

ANGRY EYES

We know now how to keep a healthy amount and level of eye contact. How can we read the eyes to know when someone is just furious with us? Sure, some people will give off other signs of anger (because, remember, body language is usually composed of an entire canvas of behaviors)—but some people are very good at camouflaging their unspoken signals. If your girlfriend says she isn't angry—but you know darn well that she is . . . or at least you think she is . . . how can you tell for sure? (And just to be clear, men can be as good as women at hiding their true feelings.) If you can read her eyes, you can get a pretty good idea of what's happening in her head. What are you looking for?

The eye blinks. As we discussed in the previous section, excessive eye blinking can be a sign of stress, anxiety, or lying. (If you've made her really mad, she may be feeling all of these emotions at once.)

Wide eyes. Our eyes naturally pop open when we're very angry, excited, or terrified. If she's got bulging eyes and they're fixed on you, you're in the doghouse for sure.

Dilated eyes. Another sign of nervousness or excitement, and something that's completely out of our control. Thus, a very good indicator of someone's state of mind.

Narrow eyes. You thought you were safe because her eyes aren't ready to fall out of her head? Well, eyes that are narrowed to slits send a signal that she's not on board with what you're saying. She's either up in the air, deciding whether you're telling her the truth, or she's sure that you're lying to her.

The stare. She won't look away from you after you've done something to make her angry. You're going to want to interpret this not as an overture to romance, but as a sign of hostility.

The eyebrows. An obvious sign of displeasure, the furrowed, frowning, or knitted eyebrows mean that you're probably in some sort of trouble with your lady (though these eyebrows can also signal confusion—as though she just doesn't understand you at all). One raised eyebrow indicates that she doesn't believe a word coming out of your mouth.

Her eye contact. If she's telling you she's not angry but she won't look you in the eye while she says it . . . you know what that means.

Her eye contact, part 2. She's staring at the wall while you offer up a lame excuse. She's finished listening to you at this point.

Rolling, rolling, rolling. Did she just roll her eyes at you? That means she's fed up. Abort the conversation for now and try again later.

Interpreting eye contact is an important part of evaluating our daily conversations, as we can see from the example of the angry girlfriend. She's saying one thing with her words, yet her eyes are telling us a completely different story. The same is true for the rest of our relationships, whether they're personal, work-related, intimate, or casual: The message coming from the eyes is often the clearest indication of who—and what—we're dealing with.

CHAPTER FOUR: Now that we understand that the eyes reveal more than we may want them to, we need to understand what the rest of the face is saying. What does it mean, for example, when your mother purses her lips? What signal are you sending when you yawn uncontrollably? And what about blushing? The face is a relatively small area of the body, and yet, we must understand each part of it to fully comprehend its role in body language. In this chapter, we'll discuss some of the most common facial cues and learn what they mean in terms of deciphering the messages behind them.

FACE FIRST!

Our face is our identity. We're recognized by the shape of it, by the nose in the middle of it, by the lips towards the bottom of it, and by how all the different aspects of our face come together (and remember, first impressions are based on appearances). Are we beautiful, or plain? Do our facial tics come across as being aggressive or rather submissive? These things are largely out of our control—unless we have plastic surgery to up our beauty quotient, or we take the time to learn what we're saying with our faces . . . without ever uttering a word.

The Shape of Things

Although many of us like to think we're above judging people by their looks, we're probably not as innocent as we think we are. Did you ever see someone and just get a bad feeling about them—without ever having any real interaction with them? Did you ever realize that you harbored hostility towards a person you didn't even know? Or on the flip side, have you ever had a warm, trusting feeling about a complete stranger just because he or she looked like a nice person? (Salespeople count on you feeling this way, which is part of the reason attractive people in sales tend to do quite well.)

Without realizing it, we're reacting to someone's physical attractiveness—or lack of it—and responding at the most visceral level. We may even go so far as to react to the shape of a person's face, preferring long faces to short ones, or fat faces to skinny faces.

When we see a face we're attracted to, neurons fire in a part of our brain that creates a warm, excited feeling in our bodies, further attracting us to this person who makes us feel good physically.

While different people find different facial types attractive, as a society, we tend to agree that well-formed, symmetrical, youthful faces without obvious flaws are the most beautiful. Men and women who fit this description are more likely to be accepted by others, to be perceived as being truthful, and to generally get by nicely in life without ever running into the kind of discrimination that less attractive people may deal with on a regular basis.

Now, while it's true that personality can actually make or break a person's experience in life (a gorgeous woman with no personality may seem less attractive to those who know her, while a physically unattractive person with a booming zest for life may overcome the physical judgment he's up against), the fact is, the prettier you are, the better shot you have in life to begin with. You simply won't have to clear the hurdle of non-beauty and its effect on the way people judge you.

Shootin' Blanks

We've discussed the blank face a bit already, noting that it's often a sign that someone is completely disinterested in what their partner is saying to them. Some people have medical conditions that leave them without expression. These people are often perceived as having something seriously wrong with them—and this, in turn, affects the amount and quality of their daily interactions.

Think about how facial expressions play a major role in even the most minor connections. Let's say you walk into the post office and smile at the postman working behind the desk. He, in turn, is kind to you. Maybe he even offers up a joke or an anecdote about his day, which gives you the chance to laugh with him or otherwise enter into a conversation—all of which started with the simple gesture of a smile.

The person with a blank face—also called a "flat affect"—is often shut out of even the most basic social interplay, which can have a negative effect on their self-esteem and lead to a lifetime of shyness, seclusion, and general depression.

So what's the point? If you don't have a blank face you don't have to worry about this, right? You can smile all you want, and people are going to love you for it. True enough. This is just an example of the power of facial expressions— or the lack of them—that we seldom take the time to acknowledge. Recognizing that our faces often unwittingly say more about us than we know is a major step in controlling our body language.

THE NOSE

The nose basically betrays an unspoken message in two ways: by flaring and crinkling.

One of your male coworkers is always hitting on the ladies in the office. He approaches the desk of a shy female employee and starts working his magic (or so he thinks). She never looks up at him (indicating she's not really interested in what he's saying; eye contact is discussed in Chapter Three), and you notice that she's crinkling her nose. The message? She thinks this guy stinks—not in the literal sense (unless he bathes in cologne each morning as part of his mating ritual).

So he struck out with that one. He moves on to the desk of a rather assertive female, who returns his propositioning with a glare (ooh ... things aren't looking good for him—glares are also discussed in Chapter Three). In addition, her nostrils are flaring, which is a sure sign that she is not happy. Expect to see him tossed across the office in about two seconds.

LIP SERVICE

You're concentrating intently on the instructions for installing your new DVD player. Quick! What's your mouth doing? Is it screwed up tight, or is it smashed into a tight line across your jaw? Is your tongue hanging out because your mouth is wide open? We seldom think of the lips in terms of body language—probably because the lips are, of course, associated with verbal messages—but we can learn a lot from a person's mouth, even when they remain completely silent.

In fact, the lips may say more about what we're truly think-ing and feeling than any other body part!

It's Like a Tightrope!

Your boss has called a last-minute meeting and is seated at the head of the conference room table with his lips pressed together so hard, you wonder if he's going to be able to sepa-rate them or if they've fused into one rather skinny lip.

You'd better get yourself some coffee, because you're probably in for a long meeting. Something's definitely wrong, and you can tell just by looking at the man's mouth. He's incredibly tense. His lips ain't movin', but they're telling you the whole story anyway.

Be aware that in another situation, this lip maneuver can signal other emotions, such as:

→ Anger

→ Frustration

→ Sadness

→ Disagreement

→ Confusion

So before you pin the "tense" label on someone with tight lips, you'd do well to assess the entire situation. When your mother is baking a pie from scratch and her lips are pressed together in this fashion, it may just mean that things aren't going as well as she'd hoped—she's a bit frustrated, but not quite ready to blow a gasket.

Is That My (Lip) Purse?

Now, there's a difference between the tense-lip display and the classic pursing of the lips. Where smashing your lips together into one thin line usually signals some sort of distress, pursing the lips (which is more like rolling your lips around, sticking them out, or puckering them for effect) tells the other person that you are in direct opposition to whatever it is he's saying. You may not believe him or you may not see his point of view. Then again, you might be mulling over what he's saying.

The lip curl, of course, is quite different from the lip purse or the use of the tight-lipped expression. Curling the lip is usually done in response to something we find distasteful or disgusting.

The lip purse is a classic sign of defiance or confusion. Teenagers have to perfect this move before they're allowed to graduate from middle school. (No, not really, but they're the world champs at this antagonistic lip move.) If you regularly have disagreements with an officemate or with your spouse, take special note of what he or she does with those lips during your next go-round. Stop the conversation as soon as those lips start putting on a show and say, "I can tell by the way you're pursing your lips that you and I are not seeing eye-to-eye on this issue. What, in particular, do you not agree with?" With any luck, you'll throw the other person so off balance with your assessment of their body language that you'll have no trouble winning the argument. (Are you starting to see how useful body language can be?)

Pouty Mouth

What does the sad mouth tell us? Well, obviously, it can signal distress and grief. Kids everywhere do the pout very well, and it most often lets a parent or teacher know that there is something amiss in this young person's life.

You may be surprised to learn that pouting is also sometimes an indication of tension, as when you find yourself pouting when nothing is going right—you're behind in your work, the weather is lousy, and you're coming down with a cold. You're not really sad, you're just frustrated and possibly angry.

Pouting signals more than sadness. People who are embarrassed about something they've done will often pout their troubles away.

The pout is even common during courtship. Jutting the lower lip out makes us look child-like, you see, which means we're really innocent and just looking for someone to care for us. (Another kind of creepy aspect of body language, but you probably know someone who insists on pouting around members of the opposite sex.)

So the next time you see an adult wearing a pout, don't assume that he is about to fall apart crying—it could be that he's having a rotten day . . . or he's ashamed of himself . . . or he's in love. Watch for other body language cues to find out why that lower lip is sticking out before you offer condolences—or congratulations.

The Smile

We discussed the smile briefly in Chapter One. What you need to know is that there are real smiles and fake smiles. Real smiles, obviously, are a genuine expression of happiness or pleasure. You can detect a real smile by observing a person's crow's feet (or, in the case of a younger person, the outside corners of the eyes). The muscles in this area contract when a real smile is being offered. The corners of the mouth also move upward—as opposed to laterally in a fake smile. The underlying message: This person is happy to see you.

You're right to be wary of a less-than-genuine smile that's being offered to you, especially in a business setting. This person probably has ulterior motives of some sort (whether he's out-and-out lying to you about the price of your car repair or just trying to get you to think he's a swell guy so that you won't have a fit when he tells you that your car is no longer under warranty). It's fine to return the courtesy, but be on guard and prepared to stand your ground.

Smiling is directly related to an elevation in mood. Faking a smile can lead you into a real smile, so don't fight it when you're feeling blue. Try a phony smile when you're having a terrible day and gauge how it affects your outlook. You may just find you're feeling better, despite your best intentions to stay down in the dumps.

If someone is offering you a fake smile in a social situation, don't offer up your entire life's story. This other person may be kind enough, and in time you may come to know her better—but for now, keep a healthy distance.

DOWN UNDER

While the lips have a story all their own to tell when we discuss body language, the lower half of the face—the jaw and the chin—are busy sending their own signals. Impossible, you say? They're just bones—how can they do anything that isn't under our complete control? Well, those bones are connected to muscles, which are connected to the brain, which is completely out of our control when it comes to body language.

Jaw Breaker

Whether we are aware of it our not, our jaw line is something that we are judged on. We may have a receding jaw, a protruding jaw, or one that's just right (by society's standards, that is). There are also square jaws, which, although rather uncommon, are usually seen as a sign of physical strength. Generally speaking, a protruding jaw gives the impression that its owner is somehow a lesser person—something that goes back to how we judge one another based on the perception of body parts.

The jaw also plays an important part in conveying certain emotions. Picture someone who is completely terrified—what is their mouth doing? It's wide open, with the jaw dropping in horror. Dropping the jaw in this way can also signify surprise or a sudden thrill. In some cases, the jaw drop is associated with bewilderment (as when you don't see your pay raise reflected in your check for the umpteenth consecutive week—your mouth dropped just thinking about it, didn't it?).

Keep in mind that the jaw drop doesn't indicate that the mouth is wide open. It can be just a slight opening of the mouth, accompanied by other body language signaling that this person is experiencing some sort of emotional experience.

When you see someone's mouth hanging open, you can usually discern the cause—obviously, if the person is fearing for her life, she's going to exhibit other body language signals reflecting that fear. The same can be said for a person experiencing surprise, excitement, or confusion.

What bearing does this have on your life? Well, let's say you're working with a new partner on a big project at work. It's crucial that you get her up to speed right away on what you've been doing so that the two of you can forge ahead and meet your tight deadline. You've explained everything she needs to know, and now she's wandering around the office with a strange look on her face . . . and her mouth open. This girl is lost, and you'd better make darn sure that she truly understands what you've told her, or you'll be carrying the load yourself.

The Chinny-Chin-Chin

What does the chin have to say about your personality? A lot, if you find yours pointing toward the ceiling at times. Sticking the chin out while holding the head back is a sign of arrogance and/or dominance (this is opposed to the quick thrust that is sometimes used as an unspoken greeting). Turn on the news and observe a dictator or a military commander watching his troops march by. His head will be thrust slightly backward, and his chin will be protruding outward. He's the most powerful man in the world as far as he's concerned, and this is his way of showing us.

Now, while you have the TV on, find an old movie and observe how the heroine employs the chin-toward-the-ceiling movement. In her case, it's a sign that she perceives herself as nothing less than royalty. Yes, she is (or was) better than other people, and her chin thrust is her way of conveying that message.

You'd be wise not to employ this move in everyday life. It's become such a stereotypical sign of arrogance that it's laughable—and something that other people definitely pick up on. It's one thing to use your chin to do your talking if you actually are the most powerful person in the room—

but it's quite another to try to use it otherwise. You can't fake this one and convince other people that because you can thrust your chin skyward that you actually are a force to be reckoned with; you've got to have the goods to back it up before you work it into your body language repertoire.

YAWN!

You're giving a big presentation at work. You've put many, many hours into this project and it's pretty impressive, if you do say so yourself. Halfway through your spiel, you look around and notice that people are yawning. Everyone is yawning. You try to liven things up by discussing budget cuts and the bottom line, and the yawning only increases. Must you do a tap dance in order to hold the attention of this group?!

While yawning is traditionally interpreted as a sign of fatigue or boredom, it can also signal a case of nervousness. You need to back up and think about what you've been telling these people. Are they in danger of losing their jobs? Are they going to work more for less money? Are big changes coming down the pike? The yawning may have started as a response to less-than-favorable news.

Of course, the interesting thing about yawning is that it spreads like a pox. One guy yawns, and then the guy across the table from him yawns, and then the gal at the end is yawning . . . sometimes it can get so out of hand that people who were not the least bit fatigued find themselves completely exhausted just from being in the company of yawners. What's worse, it's almost impossible to stop yourself from yawning.

Why do we yawn when we feel tense? Physically, tension produces adrenaline, which causes the oxygen level in the bloodstream to decrease. Yawning brings more oxygen in and helps us to refuel the bloodstream.

The next time you're assessing someone who is seemingly bored by what you're saying, or the next time you find yourself yawning when you know you've had a good night's sleep, pay attention to what else may be going on. Is it possible that you're locked in an uncomfortable conversation or situation? You may be more tense than you even realize—and since yawning is commonly perceived as a sign of boredom, your continued inability to stop yourself from doing it may be making matters worse between you and whomever you're speaking with. Take five. Get some fresh air, clear your head, and go back to the conversation fresh. This will help even if you're truly yawning from fatigue.

BLUSHERS

Some people blush whenever they feel the slightest twinge of anxiety, discomfort, or anger—and the blushing is often not limited to the cheeks. You may feel your ears getting red, along with your neck. Some serious blushers even turn red on their chests or develop red patches on their back and torso.

For those of us who rarely feel our cheeks turning pink—no matter how bad the situation at hand may be—it may be difficult to empathize with coworkers, family members, or friends who regularly go red in the face. We may think that it's no big deal or that it's something the blusher should just learn to control through relaxation techniques.

Well, the fact is that blushing can be very embarrassing—which only tends to make matters worse (as blushing is usually a reaction to an embarrassing or tense situation to begin with). Knowing that you're turning pink in front of other people tends to make a blusher very self-conscious, which adds fuel to the fire, so to speak.

Why do some people blush all the time, while others never seem to respond to any stress in this manner? It has to do with our physical makeup. Blushing is a response of the sympathetic nervous system (specifically, its fight-or-flight response, wherein we feel the adrenaline rush during a tense situation and our body responds by preparing to defend itself). A person who turns red during a tense situation might be able to learn to control his blushing a bit, but he may never be able to eliminate it altogether. It's simply what his nervous system is programmed to do.

You'll probably never see an overtly hostile or antagonistic person blush—his nervous system is programmed to respond to stress much differently. (Where the blusher feels as though he's on the defensive, the hostile guy is on the offensive.)

READING A CHILD'S FACE

Children are often easier to read because they haven't learned to manipulate their body language, much of which, as you'll remember, is thought to be innate. (That is, it comes from our ancestors, and we have very little control over the signals we send, especially when we have no idea that we're sending any signals at all.)

When you ask your child a question, how will you know if he's telling you the truth? Children who don't believe the words coming out of their own mouths are often terrible little liars. Look for these cues when you're deciphering fact from fiction regarding who broke your heirloom vase:

Eye contact. If he's avoiding looking at you, he's probably hiding something.

Touching. An innate response to lying is called self-touching, which is supposed to comfort us in times of anxiety. Touching the mouth is thought to be the definitive sign of a liar—it's as though the liar is trying to stop the untruth from escaping.

The lips. Is he pursing them, compressing them, or doing something strange with them? It's as though he's physically trying to control the false words from slipping out.

His voice. Not really a body language cue, but a good tip: Lying kids will often stutter or trip over their words.

Now, remember, these are guidelines. You're looking for patterns in your child, so if he normally never makes eye contact with you, you can't really use that against him now. Just tune in to his signals, and before long, you'll be able to notice the discrepancies in his words and his facial cues.

grand gestures

CHAPTER FIVE: Gestures are a big part of body language—and often come to be part of our identity (along with our faces and other movements). Extroverts, for example, are constantly "talking" with their hands, as opposed to shy people, who seldom use sweeping gestures to make a point. At times, we may be confused about why someone would allow their hands to communicate so much of a message when the spoken word is just as effective—or is it? This chapter will discuss some fairly common gestures in an effort to get to the bottom of what they really mean.

TALKING WITHOUT SAYING A WORD

One of the most basic ideas behind the study of body language is that the body's movements always communicate the real truth of a situation, no matter what the mouth is saying (and whether or not we're intentionally telling a fib). Do you know what your gestures are telling the people around you? The following quiz asks about the meaning behind some of the gestures we see every day.

1. You're a woman seated in a restaurant with a blind date. You're extending your arms as you talk, and maybe twisting and crossing them in an X-like fashion as you speak. What is this telling your date?

    a) That you're defensive.

    b) That you're interested.

    c) That you pulled a muscle working out.

Answer: b. Showing off your feminine arms is a way to accentuate the difference between yourself and the male gender.

2. Your spouse has his arms crossed as you're discussing where you should eat dinner tonight. What kind of reaction should you expect from him?

    a) "I hate the place you've picked out!"

    b) "Whatever, hon."

    c) "I'm not in the mood."

Answer: Actually, any one of these answers might come out of his mouth. Crossing the arms has long been considered a defensive move, but in reality, some people just like to cross their arms.

3. You're considering buying a car from your friend. She swears it's in great shape. You notice that she reaches back to rub her neck while she lists the car's best features. What does this indicate?

    a) That she's lying.

    b) That she's telling the truth.

    c) That she has no idea what she's talking about.

Answer: a or **c**. She may not be actively lying, but she surely doesn't have all the information you need. This move is usually a signal of confusion.

4. Your officemate has thrown together a presentation that will affect both of your jobs. You're freaking out; he's sitting back with his hands behind his head, telling you everything's fine. Should you trust him?

    a) Yes

    b) No

Answer: a. The hands-behind-the-head move is a classic sign of confidence. If you normally trust him, you can stop worrying.

5. When trying your best to convince someone to see your point of view, your hand gestures should be:

    a) Mainly palms-down.

    b) Mainly vertical.

    c) Mainly palms-up.

Answer: c. Facing your palms to the ceiling shows that you're non-threatening and willing to work with the other person. Palms-down gestures are a sign of dominance.

6. You're rubbing your eye as you're speaking to your boss. What nonverbal message are you sending?

    a) You're nervous.
    b) You're lying.
    b) You love your job.

Answer(s): **a** and/or **b.** Self-touches are usually the result of feeling anxious. Your boss may be an intimidating sort or you may be telling a white lie (sure, that report will be on his desk at the end of the day).

7. You ask your neighbor if he knows who's been stealing your newspaper. He shakes his head back and forth so quickly, you think it might be on a tightly wound spring. Is he telling you the truth?

    a) Yes
    b) No

Answer: Probably **b.** Shaking or nodding one's head in this manner is usually a nervous reaction to something—so although he may not be the culprit, he may know who is.

8. You're seated across the table from a date who can't stop fidgeting in his seat. What should you glean from this body language?

    a) He's bored.
    b) He's nervous.
    c) He's uncomfortable.

Answers: It could be any one of these things. Remember, the key to deciphering body language is first knowing what's normal for the other person and then placing the behavior in context.

The concepts behind the questions and answers to this quiz are discussed in further detail in this chapter.

HEADY MATTERS

We move our heads so much that we probably hardly notice when we're doing it. Our noggin is really as expressive as our face when it comes to body language—and what we do with it can either emphasize what we're saying or can contradict it completely. Pay attention to how often you nod at people or how you tilt your head—these movements are often the period at the end of our spoken sentences.

Nodding and Shaking

You know these moves. Up and down for yes, and side to side for no. Have you ever seen a friend say yes while she shakes her head no? You can't believe that someone would make this error—obviously, she meant to nod . . . or did she? Nodding and shaking the head are such automatic reflexes that we usually believe the head movement over a contradictory spoken message—because nobody does mix up their nodding and shaking.

Nodding has several different meanings. We nod in agreement during our conversations, we nod to say hello, and we might even nod when we're thinking about something. Sometimes, one strong nod is used to underscore our own belief in what we're saying (a way of saying, "So there!").

Shaking the head, meanwhile, tends to mean that we're in disagreement or disbelief about something we've seen or heard. People also tend to use the head shake when they are sympathizing with others (which is a way of saying, "I can't believe this is happening to you").

Tilt-a-Head

Tilting the head is a way to indicate compliance or friendliness. It echoes a child's innocence, and makes us look rather harmless and approachable. For this reason, the head-tilt is often used by women in the ritual of flirting, which will be discussed in greater detail in Chapter Nine.

THE ARMS

Our arms harbor our strength. We use them throughout the day for the most minuscule and the absolute largest tasks. Did you know that they are more than just functional tools? The way we present our arms can indicate how we're feeling at any given moment.

Look at Me!

For a woman, putting the arms out on display is a kind of "come-hither" gesture. In doing this, you're inviting comparison between the sexes—your arms are probably much smaller than your date's and more feminine (even if you work out regularly, you're not going to have the same kind of bulky muscles as a man, so your arms are still very feminine).

You needn't go to all the trouble of slinking those arms across a table to show them off to a prospective mate. How often do you wear a sleeveless dress or top? You're showing off your girly arms every time you slip on a tank top or a halter dress. If you notice hordes of men staring, it may just be because they're naturally drawn to your arms. (Which is interesting . . . you never really hear of anyone being an "arm man," which just goes to show that we often don't realize the subtle effects of body language.)

Bottom line: If you have a nice set of arms and you're out there on the dating scene, show 'em off. They'll never know what hit them.

Back Off . . . Or Come Here

Crossed arms are generally considered to be a sign of hostility, discomfort, anger, or anxiety. It's a form of self-touch (which we'll discuss later in this chapter) that may help to comfort someone who's feeling nervous or unhappy. The arm cross is also used by people who feel like they're the big cheese (think of your own boss when he's feeling full of himself—does he ever stand with his arms crossed and his elbows jutting straight out to the side? He's completely comfortable in the knowledge that he's the most powerful guy in the office).

It's not always so easy to decipher the crossed arms, though, because it's also simply a comfortable position for many people. Sometimes, especially while conversing with someone they don't know well, people don't know what to do with their arms—so they cross them. This shouldn't necessarily be regarded as a prelude to disagreement. If someone is really feeling hostile towards what you're saying, you'll be able to read it in their other body language signs (a tense mouth, for example, or bulging eyes). Then you can interpret the arm cross as a defense mechanism and brace yourself for whatever may follow.

The term open arms doesn't refer to someone standing with their arms out in front of them (or slightly askew to the sides), waiting for a big hug from you (though this can certainly be one interpretation of the phrase). Open arms simply aren't crossed. They may be in motion (expressing themselves through the use of other gestures), or they may be completely still. As long as the message they're conveying matches what the speaker is saying, open arms are a good indicator that this person is . . . well, open. She's welcoming. You can be sure that she will listen to what you have to say in response to her.

Interpreting arm gestures isn't as inexact as it may seem. You can generally get a good feel for hostile arm movements, which may include the arm cross or any sudden, jerky movements.

The important thing is to evaluate what the arms may be saying in conjunction with other body language signals so that you can get a fair idea of what's going on with the other person.

HAND JIVE

Few of us realize how much of our communication is done with our hands. The hands are incredibly demonstrative, indicating every emotion from anger to sadness to happiness to confusion to desperation . . . we have gestures to accompany almost anything we say (and of course, some of us talk with our hands almost nonstop).

The hands are seldom lonely or completely at rest. It's as though they need contact with something—anything—at all times. When you're not using your hands to complete some sort of task or to help you express yourself, what are they doing? Some people clasp their hands together; others engage them in seemingly mindless activities (like hair twirling or tapping them on a nearby surface). The fact is, the hands have a language all their own, which is what we'll discuss in the following section.

My Neck Is Just a Little Itchy

Picture this: Your boss has come to you looking for answers about a project you've been working on. You do your best to allay his fears, to assure him that you're the right candidate for this particular job, that you have everything under control. You're using an appropriate amount of eye contact and integrating a fair amount of genuine smiling, all the while punctuating the conversation with an eyebrow raise here and there. You're doing great. Just wait for him to leave and . . . there it is! The hand to the back of the neck. A sure sign that you are not nearly as comfortable as you have just portrayed yourself as being. One hand raised to the back of the head or neck can signal a host of emotions, such as:

→ Confusion

→ Discomfort

→ An opposing viewpoint

→ Animosity

→ Disappointment

Notice none of these are good feelings. No one raises a hand to the back of the neck when they're elated—unless the excitement causes a sudden flare-up of a prior neck injury that requires intermittent massaging.

I'm Just Holding Up My Big Head

Two hands behind the head signals quite a different message—one that says, "I am so comfortable in who I am and what I'm doing, I could not care less about what anyone else thinks." You can picture this gesture in your mind—and you can probably picture someone you know who either does this on a fairly regular basis, or is a perfect candidate for working this into his daily routine.

Again, people with sore necks are immune from scrutiny when they display this particular movement.

Flip 'Em Up . . . Flip 'Em Down

A palm pointing downward is a sign of dominance. If you've ever shaken the hand of someone who insists on offering his hand to you in a horizontal, palms-down position, you probably took note of it, because it's not the way most people shake—which is exactly what the shaker had in mind. This was his way of telling you, "I'm a big gun. Don't forget it." Likewise, when someone talks with their hands pointing downward, he feels very strongly about what he's saying and is less likely to be open to your conflicting ideas.

A palm facing upward is a gesture of goodwill. Like the palms-down gesture, most people don't shake hands this way, so you'll remember anyone who offers you a palm-up hand. In conversation, someone who gestures with their palms directed toward the ceiling is thought to be a sort of mediator, interested in bringing people together. This person is eager to engage in conversation with you, rather than simply letting you know her feelings on a particular issue.

Where might you be able to put the palms to use? Anywhere you're interested in conveying your particular stance. If your wife complains that you never listen to her opinions, try the palms-up approach the next time you two have a face-to-face powwow. It shows that you are listening, and that you welcome her input. If you're constantly feeling intimidated by someone, on the other hand, use the palms-down technique. You'll send the message that you're not backing down from your viewpoint just because the other person says you're wrong.

Let Your Hands Do the Talking

Aside from the less-obvious meaning behind some of our hand gestures, the hands also participate in daily communication in ways that we all understand, such as:

The fist. Almost always a sign of aggression, as when an angry person balls up his fist and bangs it on the table, or when someone is so frustrated, she just stands there clenching and unclenching her fists in an attempt to regain her composure. The fist can also be used as a way of claiming victory. You might see sports fans thrusting their fists into the air during a heated contest.

Time-out. Crossing the hands in a T-like shape indicates that another person needs to stop talking (or really does indicate the need for a time-out during a game).

The salute. The salute, of course, comes from military use, but we use it in everyday life to indicate our acknowledgment that someone else is the boss.

Knocking on wood. A clear indication that despite our savvy sense of self, we're still superstitious at heart.

Hand cupped to the ear. Indicates that we can't hear what another person is saying.

The wave. Hello or goodbye.

The OK sign, which obviously means that someone or something meets with our approval.

The peace (or "victory") sign.

The gun. Kids often use a forefinger and thumb to indicate the presence of a weapon during a game of cops and robbers. We adults use this same motion as a greeting or as a way of saying, "Nice job."

Finger "cut" across the throat. Big trouble. You're dead, figuratively speaking.

Crossing the fingers. For luck. Some people will also cross various other body parts in an attempt to increase their fortune.

Hand to the ear with pinky and thumb extended. Tells someone to give a call or that they have a call waiting for them.

Holding hands. A sign of love or affection.

High-fives. Indicates camaraderie or victory.

Of course, there are many other hand gestures that people use every day. They're as much a part of our language as the spoken word.

HIGH-FIVE

What do our individual fingers say to other people? Plenty. We have five on each hand, all of which are communicating (at least in conjunction with the other four) some type of unspoken, yet widely understood message—which can vary widely from culture to culture (something we'll discuss in Chapter Eight). For now, it's enough for us to have a refresher course on the things we do with our fingers in this culture, just in case the meaning behind the gesture has been lost over the years.

Where Is Pointer?

First, we have the forefinger. It points. It waggles. It gets in your face. It's so small, and yet so useful in everyday communication.

The Point. Obviously, we understand when someone is pointing out something to us that we're supposed to look at. The point can also be used to indicate to someone else that you're watching them, or that you're mocking them (which is why your mother always told you that it's rude to point).

The Waggle. Everyone had a teacher who held up her index finger and wiggled it from side to side as a way of saying, "Oh, no, you don't." Another interesting way to convey shame upon another person is to use both index fingers, pointing both at whomever is to be shamed, and to rub one on top of the other, probably in conjunction with saying, "Tsk, tsk, naughty, naughty."

The In-Your-Face. No doubt about this: When you use your index finger to punctuate your sentences when you're upset or angry, the other person gets your message loud and clear. This is a definite sign of anger or hostility.

Number one. Sports fans everywhere love this signal so much that they buy huge foam rubber fingers to get their point across.

Obviously, the forefinger can be involved in many other activities, such as hair-twirling or touching the face, which will be discussed in the section on self-touching.

Moving on Down the Line

Then we have the middle finger. We all know that using it by itself shows our contempt for or displeasure with another person.

The pinky is sometimes used to show arrogance, as when a lady sips her tea and intentionally raises her pinky. This is another learned body language trait, and not likely to convince anyone that you are, indeed, part of the aristocracy. (Of course, the pinky does naturally tend to stick out when you're drinking from a cup with a small handle—but there's really no need to exaggerate the motion.)

And … back to the thumb, which is famous for its up-and-down gesturing. Just about everyone knows that the thumbs-up sign indicates that we find something favorable, while giving something the thumbs-down signifies that we think it stinks. This gesture has its roots back in ancient gladiator fights. Today, of course, we use it to encourage one another or to discourage someone from pursuing an idea or an action.

There are many more body language signals that we convey through the use of our fingers and hands, some of which are uniquely our own (do you make a little "walking" motion with your forefinger and middle finger to indicate that someone should walk away from you?). The meaning behind these motions are different, depending on which culture you're dealing with, so before you use them in a foreign country, do your research (and read Chapter Eight in this book).

SELF-TOUCHES

Rubbing the eyes. Wringing the hands. Rubbing the chin. Look around: People everywhere are engaged in these self-touches. Do you ever wonder why we do these things? What do they mean?

Many of these movements are self-comforting measures that we employ when we're feeling anxious, frightened, or are engaged in deep thought. Someone who is rubbing his chin, for example, may be in his own little world, thinking about what he's going to do once he escapes his cubicle for the evening—or he may be worried about the accounting error he made which he will have to explain to his supervisor.

These activities tend to become more pronounced when we're highly emotional. Wringing the hands, for example, is a classic sign of worry. People who absent-mindedly scratch their arms are generally believed to be anxious about something. People who suffer from mental illness often engage in a series of destructive self-touches (pulling their hair out, for example, or scratching themselves till they bleed).

These touches are another outlet of the sympathetic nervous system's fight-or-flight response to stress and are mostly used as a means of comforting ourselves. However, some of these movements can also signal that someone is anxious because he's lying, something we'll discuss in more detail in Chapter Ten.

JIGGLES, TWITCHES, AND NERVOUS HABITS

Maybe you know someone who is constantly dancing around while you talk to him, jiggling his feet while he's at his desk, and shuffling around in his seat. What the heck is wrong with this guy—is he harboring some deep, dark secrets? Is he merely insecure? Should you tell him that you know he's hiding something in an effort to make him confess all?

Sometimes nervous habits are just that—habits born of a nervous disposition (some people are just naturally more anxious than others) or they can even be physical adaptations to certain situations. People may shuffle their feet because their shoes are too tight or because they have back pain when they stand too long. Your pal may have started doing that jiggling-the-foot thing out of boredom at some point and found that it's pretty soothing. Maybe he's shuffling in his seat because he's uncomfortable.

At other times, of course, nervous wiggling and twitching are clear indicators that something's amiss. When your coworker is confronted with some creative accounting that he's done, does he tap his fingers nervously on his legs? Are his feet tapping and/or shaking? Is he blinking like mad? What about his nodding? Nodding, as though in agreement, can be a sign of anxiety if it's done at rapid-fire speed.

What you really need to know about nervous twitches is this: If a normally nervous person exhibits signs of anxiety after being accused of lying or stealing, you're going to have to dig deeper for the truth than merely observing how his body reacts to the allegation. If someone who is a stone fox reacts to an accusation by becoming a live wire or a bundle of nerves, however, you can be fairly certain that he is hiding something.

take a stance—carefully

CHAPTER SIX: Since we're discussing body language, it's about time we get around to addressing the actual body. The way we carry and position ourselves have a great bearing on how others perceive us. We can know everything about controlling our eye contact and cutting down on the more aggressive (or passive) hand gestures, but if we don't know how to use the body to our advantage, we're missing out on a major aspect of nonverbal communication.

STANDING TALL

The way we use our bodies sends a clear message to others in the room. We have to be concerned with posture, as well as open and defensive stances. Then there's the matter of personal space—are we intruding on someone else's turf? How will he or she react to this? Holding our bodies correctly can make us look like winners—or losers. We'd best get down to business so that we come out on the right side of this equation.

Stand Up Straight!

What did your mother always tell you? Don't slouch. Slouching only makes you look like you have the weight of the world on your shoulders. It makes you look depressed, as though you're lacking life, and also makes your body appear smaller (which is not a good thing, and you'll find out why in the next section). Adopting a slouched position with your head down and your hands jammed into your pockets sends a message to other people that says you're unhappy and not strong enough to tackle the challenges of everyday life.

On the other hand, standing up nice and tall has other benefits besides making you look like you're in contention for some sort of modeling contest. A shoulders-back, head-held-high stance exudes an air of confidence, as though you actually can handle whatever life is going to throw your way.

Animals do anything they can to make themselves appear larger to potential predators—humans do something similar by using their shoulders to appear as wide as possible, so the taller you stand and the broader you can make your shoulders appear, the better protected you'll be from potential predators in your own life.

Aside from standing tall, there are basically two categories of posture and body positions: those that express a laid-back attitude, and those that express a sense of urgency. Postures that fall into the first category might include leaning back in a chair during a closed-door meeting that has a relaxed atmosphere. A posture that falls into the second category might include the way you lean forward on the conference table while explaining the need to address a particular issue before the close of the business day.

Each way of posturing is completely appropriate in the right setting, but imagine what would happen if you took the laid-back posture into a crucial meeting: You'd be perceived as arrogant, rude, and lazy. And if you brought your rather demanding posture into a relaxed meeting, you might be looked at as being tightly wound and in serious need of some time off. These seem like obvious mistakes that you would never make—and yet, people do things like this all the time. Their posture sends the wrong message, which causes other people to assume certain things about their character. Right or wrong, this goes on every day in offices (and in homes, during personal interactions) across the country. It's such an easy thing to rectify—so make sure you're using your posturing appropriately.

Defense

Let's say you see two coworkers, Brad and Gail, having a discussion across the way from where you're perched (apparently with some free time on your hands, as you're able to watch the entire interaction). Now, these two people are on relatively equal footing in the office and often work together on projects, so seeing them together doesn't immediately make you think that anything is up—except you notice that while Gail is standing with her feet planted wide and her hands on her hips with her elbows sticking straight out from her sides, Brad is slouching with his hands in his pockets and his legs crossed at the ankle. His arms are also crossed. While Gail is speaking to him, he stares down at the floor, as though he's lost in thought.

What have you just observed? A friendly discussion or a heated, one-sided debate? From what we can see, it would appear that Gail is quite upset about something and that Brad is feeling a bit defensive about it. How can you tell? By the way he made himself look smaller by slouching (as though he's the prey hiding from the predator), and also by the way he avoided making eye contact. Gail, on the other hand, made herself appear large enough with her feet planted wide—she made herself appear even larger by placing her hands on her hips and pointing her elbows straight out—now she's taking up a maximum amount of space.

So what are some of the classic defensive postures? People usually look for something that includes the arm cross, though as we've discussed earlier in this book, crossing the arms isn't always a sign of defensiveness. Sometimes it's just comfortable. Same thing with crossed legs—some people just cross them out of habit, whether they're feeling open or closed off to someone else's argument. We can say that someone who is feeling defensive may be likely to cross the arms or legs, almost as though he is trying to protect himself from your opinion, but that you shouldn't assume that because your husband is sitting in the living room with his legs crossed that he's ready for a fight. (In this case, it's a fairly sure bet that Brad is using the leg cross as a way to shut himself off from Gail.)

Come to Me!

What are the postures that say, "Hey, I'm open to you"? Sitting with your legs uncrossed, even askew. Crossing the legs can be an inviting position, as long as you're angling yourself toward the person you're speaking to. Standing with your feet apart is thought to be a welcoming— although somewhat dominant—posture, as is almost any posture involving uncrossed (or "open") arms.

Leaning in toward whomever you are speaking with is something that invites the other person into your little world, or shows them that you want to be inside theirs. Mimicking their posture (or movement) with yours is also something that shows the other person that you're open to what they're saying—but take it slowly. You're not playing a game of monkey-see, monkey-do. You're simply observing what the other person is doing and subtly following suit.

For example, if you're in a conference with a representative from another company who could make or break a big deal for your company, watch what the guy does. Does he lean back in his chair? Go ahead and relax a bit (but not to the point where you look like you're not fully engaged in what he's saying). Is he leaning forward with his hands clasped on the table? You'll want to lean forward, too, and show your hands (as hiding them indicates some sort of deception on your part). Without his even realizing it, you've successfully communicated that you're on the same wavelength, and you can handle whatever this guy is ready to propose.

What's Your Angle?

This leads us to a discussion of how we angle ourselves towards other people. Using our shoulders, angling is a method of assessing how we "square" ourselves to others—do we angle toward them with our shoulders (a sign that we'd like to get to know them or converse with them), or do we angle away (a sign that we'd rather not get involved in chit-chat with them)? There are varying degrees here, which means that we might angle somewhat toward another person, but not completely—or, we can turn our back on them, which shuts them out of the angle (and our intimate audience) altogether.

It's generally agreed that the upper body does most of the nonverbal talking—especially when two people are seated. So if your coworker has his legs crossed (which is supposed to be a closed-off body language signal) but his shoulders are completely squared toward you, go with the signals you're getting from his torso: He's open to you and your ideas.

Imagine this: You've had a long day. On your way home, you pop over to your kid's soccer game, something you're actually looking forward to—except you've had an incredibly long week, you're burned out from talking to everyone in the office, and you can't imagine standing on the sidelines making small talk with the other parents you barely know for an hour or more at this point. You're probably going to pick a relatively secluded spot near the field (defining your need for a lot of personal space, which we'll discuss later in this chapter) in an attempt to shut yourself off from the masses. If this doesn't work, you may find yourself sitting three feet from someone else, but looking straight ahead at the game the entire time—you'll never turn your upper body toward anyone else, which allows you to shut them out of your world altogether. It's a weird thing some of us do all the time—combining our personal space with closed-off angling means that we can pretend we're all alone, even when we're surrounded by other people.

But what if you wanted to chat with the other parents? You'd be much more likely, at some point, to turn to them (angling yourself in their direction) and start a conversation, which would probably lead to a decrease in your personal space, as people engaged in friendly conversation naturally tend to move a bit closer to one another as the discourse continues.

Wait a minute, you say. You can certainly stand next to someone on a sideline keeping your shoulders angled to the front, and chat with the guy next to you without even looking at the person you're speaking to. That's true—but what you're saying with your body language is, "We're going to keep this conversation as short and to-the-point as possible." There's nothing really wrong with doing that, but you should be aware of the signal you're sending (in case you're left wondering why you never develop any relationships that go beyond small talk).

Walking the Walk

Your gait says a lot about how you view yourself—and plays a major role in how others view you, as well. Earlier in the chapter, we discussed standing up straight. Follow through when you start moving. When you walk, make sure that you're holding your head up, your shoulders back, and your palms are to the rear (this is a sign of dominance left over from our simian ancestors; apes hold their hands this way when they move). Your speed should be brisk but not absurdly so—walking too fast can send a signal that you're anxious; walking at a turtle's pace can make you look lazy or depressed (or completely lost in thought).

If you tend to point your toes inward while you walk, concentrate on straightening them out. Walking with the toes pointing in makes you look almost child-like and definitely less like an authoritative figure (while walking with them pointing outward can make you look intimidating). Incorporating this one little trait into your walk tells the world that you're confident and capable.

Adopting a swagger with your walk is going a bit overboard—unless you're sure you can pull it off. Swaggering (or strutting) involves a slight swaying from side to side and an exaggerated step. You're taking up more room when you walk, showing people that they had better watch out for you—which should be easy, considering that people who strut around the office or home are pretty easy to spot. This walk is associated with dominance and arrogance.

Imagine you're having dinner in a restaurant with friends. You see an average-looking guy strutting his way across the room. Your eyes are immediately drawn to him because his walk has made him noticeable. You may actually be thinking, "He's nothing special. Where does he get off walking around like that?" If you got to know this man, you'd probably find that he's very, very confident—perhaps too much so. But confidence is something that other people are drawn to, so while this man may not be model-handsome, he may have a bevy of beauties lined up who are just waiting for his call.

What kind of walk tells people to leave you alone? The slouched walk, with head down. People will assume that there's something wrong and will leave you to wallow in your sadness.

SPACE CASES

Are you offended by people who crowd your space? Ever wonder how much personal space is appropriate in different settings—and how much might send the message that you'd rather not associate with another person? Truth be told, the amount of appropriate personal space an individual needs varies from situation to situation. This section will talk about the most common interactions here and offer up some general guidelines for keeping your distance—or getting close enough for true comfort.

This Space Is My Space

Earlier, we talked about employing personal space as a way to seclude ourselves from others, using the example of a parent at a soccer game who purposefully chooses a spot on the sidelines away from everyone else. If you saw someone doing this, how would you know whether that person really wants to be left alone or is just shy? Should you leave him alone or draw him into your conversation by approaching him?

You may not know until you actually approach him. Look for other body language signs: Is he standing straight, with shoulders back, his feet planted widely, and his arms crossed, his eyes focused on nothing other than the game? These are typical signs that this person is confident but closed off at the moment. On the other hand, if he's rather slouched and seems to be looking to make eye contact with someone—anyone—you can be fairly sure that he won't refuse a friendly overture.

Of course, when in doubt, it's always best to err on the side of kindness and to assume that someone who looks intimidating and uninterested in human interaction may not be aware of the body language signals he's sending to others.

Everyday Interactions

You might love the chance to sidle up to everyone you know in order to spend some quality time with them—but do you know how much personal space other people need?

→ In an intimate situation—with your spouse or loved one—you'll want to maintain about a foot of personal space between you and the other person. (This also allows you to speak in much more hushed tones, which leads to further intimacy.)

→ With your friends or other family members, the distance can vary a little more—anywhere from twelve inches to three feet, generally speaking.

→ At a party or during a business meeting, it's wise to maintain at least two and a half to three feet between yourself and a person you don't know very well.

→ Out and about, shopping at the mall, keep a distance of at least three feet between you and a perfect stranger (and more if there's enough space to do so).

→ In an office setting, where you're setting up a workspace, it's wise to have at least six feet between desks. Cubicles provide more perceived room between work areas (and much-needed shelter from constantly having to make—or avoid—eye contact).

What should you do if someone is crowding you? Maintain eye contact and step back. Usually this is sufficient enough to reclaim your own personal territory. If the other person keeps crowding you, though, and it's appropriate to do so (as in the case of a family member who just keeps coming closer and closer . . . and closer), you may actually have to speak up and ask her to take a step back. (This won't work if you're standing on a crowded bus. Remember, these are guidelines to ensure optimum comfort, but sometimes there's simply not enough room to maintain the appropriate amount of space between parties. That's when we have to suck it up and just deal with being uncomfortable for a while.)

Women are generally more comfortable with less personal space. Men tend to strive for the outer limits of acceptable personal space. (This doesn't mean that women enjoy being crowded; it only means that close female friends can have a foot of space between them without feeling uncomfortable; close male friends will want to put all the space they can between themselves.)

It's also important to note that personal space guidelines vary from culture to culture, so if you're in a foreign country where everyone seems to be right next to you every second of the day, resist the urge to freak out—or to interpret the lack of space between you and a very handsome foreigner as some kind of marriage proposal. Cultural differences in body language are discussed in Chapter Eight.

POWER POSITIONS

Whether you're headed into a meeting or a party, you might be getting a knot in your stomach. These things never go well for you. You always end up feeling as though there was something more you could have—or should have—done, and that people don't respond well to you. How can you turn this pattern around? By positioning yourself correctly.

Don't Speak from the Rear of the Room

Is there any bigger waste of time than an ineffective business meeting? You know how things can go: People take their time coming in, take their seats around the table, and wait for someone to say something that has any relevance to anything that's going on in the office. Many times, these same people leave the conference room asking each other, "What was that all about?"

If you're in charge of leading a meeting, the big guns should not be spread out among the masses. Seat your key players where the action is, whether it's at the head of the conference table or in the front of a room. Not only is this a show of force (and unity), but everyone else will know who's going to speak. Employees won't be looking around the room at who's present and who isn't—they'll see which of the big cheeses have taken time out of their schedules for this very important gathering.

If you're just a regular Joe attending a meeting, don't take a seat right next to the chairman of the board. (You have your place, too, and it's with the rest of the employees, even if you have played golf with this guy once or twice.) Remember to use your best body language skills to look attentive and interested—sit up straight, lean in when appropriate, avoid self-touches, strive to make appropriate eye contact. These may not win you any bonus points, but adopting the wrong kind of body language—appearing bored or too relaxed—will definitely get you noticed (and not in a good way).

Follow the Leader

At a party, how can you find successful interactions? Simple. Don't shy away from the action. Position yourself where things are happening, whether it's dancing or lively conversation. Too often party poopers will complain, "No one ever talks to me at parties." Well, of course, if you've positioned yourself on the periphery of the action, no one's going to take note of you—in fact, they may assume that you're creating a huge personal space around yourself.

Next time you're at a party or in a bar, look at what the different sexes are up to. Men tend to stake out their own little spaces and move about very infrequently, while women tend to flit from space to space. These are thought to be methods of attracting the opposite sex—the man is saying, "I'll be right here all night," while the woman is checking out the prospects.

Bottom line: Jump into a social situation with both feet. That's why you're there, after all. Use your body language knowledge to send the message that you're confident and open, keeping in mind that body language can't do all the work. You'll actually have to open up your mouth at some point and engage in conversation—but as long as you're sending the right nonverbal signals, you're in the game. Go get 'em.

making contact

CHAPTER SEVEN: Touching is one of those areas of body language that confuses and excites people the most. Men and women can get themselves into a lot of trouble with their touches if they don't know how others may be interpreting them. In established relationships, meanwhile, partners can hug one another and still feel very distant. This chapter will take a look at the way we physically interact with the people in our lives in an attempt to clear up the big mysteries behind the human touch.

A LOOK AT TOUCHING

Touching and feeling are two of the most primal and powerful senses we posses. The act of touching precedes the dawn of mankind and language—it was one of the first forms of communication, so it's important for us to recognize where our touches began, what they were first intended to mean, and how this affects us today.

Touching Does the Talking

Just as we tend to believe body language over the spoken word (assuming that because someone has little control over his nonverbal messages, he can't manipulate or change it), we also tend to read into and believe touch more than any other body language signal. Not so sure you believe this? Imagine this: You've just spent an evening with a date who doesn't seem to be all that compatible with you. He barely made eye contact with you, he sat facing away from you during dinner, and on top of it, the conversation was only so-so. You're thinking that you'll never go out with him again, but on the way home, he takes your hand and holds it so nicely, so tenderly, that you start to melt. When he walks you to the door, he plants an amazing kiss on your lips and holds you tightly for a moment before he tells you he'll call you.

Of course, you spend two weeks waiting for him to call and he doesn't . . . but still, you wait. And wait. And wait. But why? If the date went so badly, why would you ever want to see him again? Because through his use of touch, he convinced you that he cared. The two of you could be intimate. Why, you could be the next great couple. Curse him and his effective use of touch!

Sound silly? Ask your friends how many guys they've dat-ed who were great kissers but not so much fun to be around. Think about how many less-than-perfect relationships you've been in where you were determined to end it, but you found yourself in the guy's arms all over again. It happens—and it happens more than we realize. Touch draws us to other peo-ple, establishing an intimacy that keeps us together.

Our fingers are filled with sensitive nerves and are our pri-mary link to the physical world. This is one reason why touch is so powerful—and one way we learn about the peo-ple in our lives. Based on others' reaction to our touches, we can tell how they feel about us. (Do they enjoy our touch-es or reel away in disgust?)

In the Beginning

From the time we're infants, we're hooked on touch. Mothers cuddle their babies, hugging them tightly at times either to express their love and concern or as a means of comforting them. In return, children hold on to or snuggle into their mother's arms, which is their way of accepting the comfort and saying, "I need you." Researchers theorize that adult hugging—although different in its intimacy—is based on these early mother-child interactions. We never outgrow the need for contact in our lives.

Research has also shown that all infants, including pree-
mies, benefit greatly from massage, which demonstrates
the healing power that touch can have. In fact, studies
have shown that children who don't receive enough physical contact in the first year of life don't grow and develop as
quickly as their cuddled peers.

What about adult hugs? They're not all created equal,
as you well know. We have different hugs for the different
people in our lives, so the hug you reserve for your mother
is not necessarily the same as the one you give your wife
after she returns from a week-long trip. An intimate hug of
this sort will leave almost no space between its participants
and will probably last longer than a less intimate embrace.

Grading the Hug

When we're first entering into a relationship, or when
we're arguing with our established partner, a hug can tell
us about the other person's feelings. Does he pull away
quickly or angle himself away from you? Things between
you probably aren't going all that well.

What are the signs that he's completely into you and
your relationship? He settles right into the hug, accepting the closeness. He doesn't hold his body away from
yours. Also, a good hug involves a slight movement
from side to side, almost as though you're rocking one
another (another way our adult hugs mimic those that
our moms gave us).

<u>WHAT YOU ALREADY KNOW</u>

You really don't need to be a body language scholar to decode a lot of the touches that we encounter each day. While there are some instances where it may be difficult to decipher someone's body cues, touch is usually a pretty good indicator of someone's intentions. (Including the guy who didn't call—his intention may have been to make you feel good about him and about yourself . . . and he did, at least temporarily.)

Touchy Feelies

Some touch cues are pretty obvious. The coworker who insists on rubbing your shoulders as you sit typing away is not just trying to be friendly. He's trying to establish an intimate bond with you. How do you know this for sure? Because as a society, we don't accept this kind of touching as "casual," and no matter what this person knows (or doesn't know) about body language, he knows that touching you in this intimate way is the first step toward sweeping you off your feet (or so he hopes). He's also as far inside your personal space as he can get, which is another sure signal that he has more on his mind than relieving your tense muscles—he wants to be in your intimate life. Make no mistake about this kind of overture. Men are also less likely to do a lot of touching (again, a society thing), so a guy who touches everyone all the time is likely looking for something, whether he knows it or not.

Less Direct Cues

However, there are all kinds of touches that we give and receive each day that are less obvious. Let's say that instead of massaging your neck for several minutes, this guy simply gives your shoulders a little rub when you greet each other. Should you let him know right then and there that you're not interested in dating him?

He might look at you a bit strangely if you do, because this kind of touching is actually socially acceptable—as long as you're comfortable with it. Short-lived touches, especially those that take place during a greeting or while saying goodbye to a person, are usually nothing more than an indication of friendly affection or politeness. This person is saying, "I like you and I'm happy to see you," or "I look forward to seeing you next time." It's a way of establishing good will between the two of you, but it doesn't cross the line into "I've got to have you in my life" territory.

Touches are often used to establish a friendly bond, which is why you'll sometimes come across someone who touches your arm as the two of you speak, or someone who smacks you on the back while the two of you share a laugh. These people are telling you that they like you and enjoy your company.

Women are more likely to "read" into touches than men are, possibly because women are more likely to touch others (and we know exactly what we mean by doing so—at least most of the time). Because we're living in a society of men and women working side-by-side, interacting with each other on a constant basis, there's been some difficulty determining harmless, appropriate touches from those that may be sexual overtures. The bottom line is that if you're uncomfortable with the way someone touches you, you have to use a strong verbal message—along with your most defensive, closed-off body language—to convey that message in no uncertain terms. The offender will get the message that you are not the least bit open to negotiation on this point.

GIMME YOUR HAND

Holding hands is usually a sign of intimacy between people, but how you hold hands with your partner says a lot about the stage and shape of your relationship. Obviously, if you're married or in a long-term relationship, hand holding may mean a lot less to you than to someone who's just starting out with a new mate. Still, it never hurts to know what your hands are saying to each other as you're walking down the street together or seated on the sofa, hand in hand, watching some tube on a boring weekend night.

Hand Holding, Part 1

You're walking down a city street with a date, feeling like this relationship has potential. Still, he's over there, and you're over here, and he's showing no signs of holding your hand.

So go ahead and take his hand. You're telling him that you're looking to move into a deeper intimacy with him. If the two of you fall into a comfortable hand holding position and he doesn't act as though he wants his hand back, you can be pretty sure that he feels the same way about you.

Long-term couples often hold hands without even thinking about how it feels. It's just natural to them, which is reflective of their level of comfort in the relationship—which can be a good thing or a bad thing, if the relationship is actually in a state of neglect. (So just because you see a couple holding hands after several years of dating, don't assume that all's wonderful on the love front. It may just be a comfortable habit for both of them.)

Hand Holding, Part 2

Now you're walking across a parking lot with a male friend. You're looking in your purse for something, and before you know it, he takes your hand and leads you to the car. What just happened here? Did the two of you cross into some level of intimacy that you weren't aware of?

Probably not. If you're observant enough in a situation like this, you'll probably notice that there was some inherent danger—maybe a car backing up, or a truck headed your way—that might have mowed you down as you looked for gum at the bottom of your bag. He would have done the same thing for his mom. He's taking care of you—perhaps because you're a woman and he's grown up believing that women need taking care of—and protecting you from harm. He's not looking to move your relationship towards marriage; he just doesn't want to scrape you up off the pavement.

Hand Holding, Part 3

You're seated across the table from your boyfriend of several months, and he reaches over to take your hand and weaves his fingers in between yours. You find this kind of irritating, actually, and a bit uncomfortable. What's he doing?

Interlocking the fingers this way sends a signal that your beau is quite taken with you and possibly ready to move your relationship forward—permanently. He's literally locking you into his hand, telling you that you're it for him. (Of course, judging from your reaction of annoyance, you may not feel the same way about him. Just be sure to let him down easy.)

Be a little wary when this hand hold is proposed to you early on in your relationship: Interlocking the fingers in this way can also be a sign of lust. He's intertwining your fingers with his just the way he'd like your bodies to intertwine. Don't go giving away the goods thinking that he's ready to pop the question. You'll end up heartbroken. Disregard the hand holding and move forward at your own pace.

Gross Grips

The hand holding was going so well . . . until you felt the sweat from your date's hand saturate your own. You cringed, faking a sneeze so that you could free yourself from the dampness of his touch. Ew.

Sweaty palms are usually due to feeling nervous, so give the guy a break. Look for other signs of nervousness, such as facial flushing or feet or legs that can't seem to stay still. Do your best to put him at ease, and you may find that those palms will dry right up. (Phew!) Sweaty palms can also be a sign of fear or stress. And of course, some people just happen to sweat more than others, so sweaty hands might be normal for him. If this is the case, you'll either learn to tolerate it or spend less time holding hands.

KISSES

Did you ever stop to wonder what kissing is all about? What would make two people want to take their mouths—which are filled with bacteria—and put them together? Nature. Kissing is basically touching—with your mouth. The area of your face right around the lips and mouth is the most sensitive. Using the lips in this way excites certain neural pathways to the brain and makes us feel good physically.

It doesn't matter which culture you find yourself in—kissing is a sign of love all over the world. So whether you're engaged in a passionate kiss in New York City or in Nepal, others will know that you are intimately connected with whomever you're locking lips with.

Kissing, of course, can be a prelude to greater intimacy. It's like a warm-up, wherein both partners are assuring each other that things are progressing normally. It's usually one of the first steps in a physical relationship, which leaves us wanting more.

TEST YOUR RELATIONSHIP BODY LANGUAGE I.Q.

Whether you're in a long-term relationship or a relatively new partnership, it can be hard to tell where your mate stands on certain issues. Disagreement is par for the course in most relationships. Learning to read your partner's body language can tell you whether this fight is just a bump in the road or a sign of a loosening connection between the two of you. Take this quiz to learn more about what body language means in your coupling.

1. At your Mom's house for Sunday dinner, where do you and your husband sit in relation to one another?

 a) Right next to each other.
 b) He sits next to your dad at one end, and you sit next to your mom at the other.
 c) He eats in the family room, watching the game, and you sit at the table.

Best answer: a. Couples who feel connected just want to be near each other, whether it's sitting next to one another, or across the table from each other. These people want to be able to see and talk to their partner, even if the room is filled with other interesting people. Sitting at opposite ends of the table or in completely separate rooms indicates that you could use a break from each other.

2. When your mate comes through the door at the end of the workday, you greet him by:

 a) Giving him a brush on the cheek.
 b) Planting a nice, long kiss on his mouth.
 c) Waving to him from your seat on the couch.

Best answer: b. It's the end of his day, and even though you may have hours of work behind and ahead of you if you're the one staying home and chasing after the kids, this is a time to re-establish your exclusive bond, the one that says you're in this life thing together. Pecking him on the cheek or giving him a brief kiss with closed, tight lips tells him that you're just going through the motions, kissing him because you think you should. And waving to him from across the room? You can do better than that.

3. When you need to talk to your wife about the monthly finances, do you:

- a) Talk to her as she's seated and you're standing.
- b) Talk to her as you're seated and she's standing.
- c) Talk to her on the same physical level.

Best answer: c. Eye contact is so important in our everyday conversations. Talking to her at eye level engages her attention; she's more likely to hear what you have to say. Conversely, engaging in an important conversation while one of you is standing above the other will only make the seated person feel as though she's being browbeaten. She'll concentrate on defending her own point of view.

4. When the two of you argue, what normally happens?

- a) He turns his back on you and talks to you as he looks out the window.
- b) You face each other and let the fireworks begin.
- c) You typically find yourself drumming your fingertips on the kitchen counter, waiting for him to get to the point.

Best answer: b. Heated arguments happen in most relationships. Facing one another and maintaining eye contact shows that you're each truly interested in what's being said. Turning your back on your partner or tapping your fingers on the table sends the message that you're incredibly bored with this conversation and that you just can't wait for it to be over.

5. You're talking to your spouse about something you think he may be guilty of (whether it's cheating on you or leaving the toilet seat up), which he denies. What are his eyes doing?

  a) They're normal-looking and one eyebrow is arched.
  b) He's blinking and his pupils are huge.
  c) He's not looking at you, so you have no idea.

Best answer: a. Arching one eyebrow means that he can't believe what you're saying (Chapter Three). Excessive blinking (also Chapter Three) and dilated pupils are a sign that he's not being completely honest, which is something we'll discuss in Chapter Ten. Avoiding eye contact altogether means that he's either completely not interested in what you're saying (Chapter Three again) or that he may not be able to look at you while he lies.

Keep in mind that body language is the study of patterns within people—so, for example, if your mate always squeezes his lips together, it's not a reliable sign of tension in him. Learning how to read your partner's body language requires a long observation of his or her behaviors prior to making any judgments.

KIDS

Should you try to decode what your children are saying to you through their body language? As long as you know the basics, it shouldn't be hard for you to read your kids. Children simply experience things and react to them—they don't stop to think about how other people will react to their reactions, which means they're very unlikely to temper their body language. If your little girl loves to snuggle with people, she's a genuinely affectionate child who needs that kind of attention. If your little boy likes to hit his pals, that's not a sign of affection—that's aggressive behavior that needs to stop.

Assessing your child's body language, more than anything else, is pure common sense. What you see is usually exactly what you're getting.

CHAPTER EIGHT: Funny thing happens when you cross over international waters and step foot on distant foreign soil: The language changes. All right, so it's not all that funny that the spoken word is unintelligible to you—but it is a little peculiar that the meaning of body language changes from culture to culture. Using the wrong gesture or trying to protect your personal space in a far-away land could get you into serious trouble with the locals, who might think you're either an ignoramus or just a typical American (which, in some countries, are interchangeable phrases).

<u>WHAT'S THE DIFFERENCE?</u>

When it comes to body language crossing borders, the differences in its meanings can be huge. Not understanding the body language of a particular country or culture can lead to real problems in your day-to-day interactions overseas, if, for example, you were to interpret someone's hostile signal as a friendly one, or unwittingly offend someone by using body language that comes across as a sexual overture or as being otherwise disrespectful.

Americans tend to be fairly ethnocentric. We like ourselves—a lot. We tend to think that so many countries want to be just like us that we needn't bother learning about other ways of life. Once you step foot on foreign soil, you have a duty to know something about the culture you're walking into. While learning the body language of another culture might seem like some kind of New Age thing to do (and you're just not into New Age stuff), it's not. Visitors to this country study the gestures we use and their meanings. We can certainly do the same.

The information contained in this chapter is an overview of some of the major differences between our body language and the body language of other cultures. It's not a complete tutorial. In other words, when you're planning your European or Asian or South American vacation, pick up a book specifically about the country you're planning to visit for more complete details on the gestures and body language used there.

Respect

How do Americans show respect to one another? (Do we ever show respect to one another?) By and large, we're a fairly laid-back culture, at least in this regard. We basically show respect for those who are more powerful than us—and even then, it's sometimes a crap shoot. For example, would you want to be a high school teacher these days? Probably not. Many teachers in the upper grades complain of the lack of respect they're shown by their students—including the way kids regularly slouch in their seats and stare out the window during lessons. (Students are better than they know at communicating through body language.)

So that narrows the field down a bit more. We tend to show respect to those who make a lot of money, or those who could somehow adversely affect our lives (a police officer, for example, is not sitting on the board of directors of some major company, but he could nail you with a ticket if you mouth off to him).

How do Americans show respect with their body language? By becoming rather submissive: by not making a lot of eye contact (which could be interpreted as a sign of intimidation); by making ourselves look smaller (not many people face off with a cop by broadening their shoulders and standing up nice and tall); and, many times, by not speaking unless it's clearly our turn, and only sparingly then.

These traits—in the United States—also tend to be associated with being fearful, which is not a trait that many Americans look kindly on—in fact, seeming too timid can be a huge detriment in this country, especially in matters of business, where it's often a kill-or-be-killed world. It's hard to live that life in the office and not have it carry over to your personal interactions, which may be why so many Americans seem hostile and disrespectful to foreigners.

Let's take the Asian culture, for example, which is largely based on respect and reserve. Where Americans typically greet one another with loud, booming hellos and hearty handshakes (or hugs), many Asians still bow to one another—which is a submissive move for each person, a way of saying, "I am no better than you"—though the handshake is also used quite frequently these days (it differs from the American version, and will be discussed later in this chapter in the section on body language and international business).

A significant difference between Asian and American cultures is the amount of respect given to the elderly. In America, it's almost nonexistent, except between family members, while in Asia, it's prevalent. This is reflected in an Asian's body language towards an older person.

Asians also tend to keep their voices low and eye contact to a minimum—a huge difference between our culture and theirs. If someone averts their eyes during a conversation, we think they're either lying to us or not listening to what we're saying, depending on who's doing the talking. We like eye contact. We expect it. If you went to Japan, though, and made direct and protracted eye contact with the local folks, you'd be perceived as discourteous.

Personal Space

In Chapter Six, we discussed personal space—how much is appropriate in different situations, why we need it, how we use it. While humans as a species are territorial and will defend their personal space when necessary, personal space varies from culture to culture, as well. As Americans, we need to have our room, even when we're among other people. In some Asian countries, though, it's not uncommon to be pushed and shoved along the city streets—and it's as natural to the culture as maintaining a healthy distance is to us. No one excuses themselves for bumping into you, just as you wouldn't apologize for keeping several feet of space between yourself and a stranger here.

This is a good example of how we could easily be offended by body language that's commonplace in another culture, because we expect people to apologize if they inadvertently push us. Someone who didn't do their research beforehand could return home from a trip to China thinking that the people are rude and hostile because of this behavior.

Mexicans, Spaniards, and many South Americans also have less stringent requirements regarding personal space and will stand very close to one another during conversation. If you didn't know the culture, you could easily mistake this as some sort of overly friendly or romantic gesture. You'd be wrong.

Touchy, Touchy

Cultures tend to be classified as either being touch-oriented or not. Americans, surprisingly enough, are classified as being not touch-oriented, even though we probably tend to think of ourselves as a fairly touchy group: We hug, we shake hands, we sometimes touch each other while talking. (But on the other hand, we love our personal space and are not always comfortable with casual touches.) The fact that we talk about and study body language only emphasizes the point that many times we have no idea what our own cultural touches mean. It would behoove any traveler, then, to have some idea of what touches mean in another culture before we lay hands on anybody.

Mexicans, for example, tend to have lingering touches. You might shake hands with a Mexican and find that he continues to hold onto your hand and your elbow for longer than feels comfortable to the average American. Mexicans tend to touch one another much more than Americans do, so your Mexican friend might, for example, rub your arm while you speak. Again, this is something that Americans might take as some kind of unspoken invitation to begin a romantic relationship, but that's just not the case. It's simply part of the culture.

Meanwhile, if you found yourself in India patting the head of a cute little child, you'd be getting yourself into hot water. In many Eastern countries, the head is considered the cleanest, most sacred part of the body (and is off-limits to the common man), while the feet are considered the lowliest and dirtiest—so you wouldn't want to nudge anybody or touch anything with your shoes or feet, lest you offend someone.

Over in Russia, you'll find family members, friends, and mere acquaintances hugging and kissing and giving the occasional hearty back slap to one another. Backing away from this kind of affection could make you look unfriendly, so when you're in St. Petersburg, be prepared to show a little love.

UNIVERSAL SIGNS

All right, so you're going to need a primer on body language before you leave the country. There's so much to know, though—aren't there some body language signals that are used everywhere, regardless of a culture's personal space requirements and their touch/don't touch policies? There are a few, and you probably already know them because we use them from time to time in our own culture. For example:

→ Waving two hands above your head and standing tall is a distress signal, telling others you need help.

→ Holding two hands to your throat signals that you're choking.

→ Tilting your head to the side, eyes closed, on top of the back of your hand means that you're tired.

→ To tell someone you're hungry, you take both hands and slap your stomach lightly.

→ Rubbing your hands together vigorously means that you're freezing or that you're very excited about something.

→ Smiles are the same everywhere.

Aren't there others, you're wondering? What about nodding? That's the same around the world, right? Well, no, it isn't. In some countries, a nod actually means no, while the side-to-side shake means yes. In other countries, the signs are completely different, though not always unrecognizable. In India, for example, one would indicate "yes" by jerking the head up and backwards or by making a figure-eight movement with the head; "no" is gestured by waving a hand back and forth (a signal that Americans interpret to mean "hello" or "goodbye").

In Asia, a common way to signify an answer in the negative is to tilt the head back and suck in air through the teeth. Asians, remember, are very reserved; they dislike conflict. This way of saying "no" is meant to soften the blow a bit.

Of course, there are other international signals—those used in diving, for example—but they won't get you very far on the streets of France. Or India. Or Bolivia. In fact, not many of these signals will be of much help at all (unless you're looking for a restaurant and pat your stomach at a passerby . . . or are hit by a moped and are able to employ the international distress signal), which is why it's so important to learn the culture, including key phrases, like, "Where is the bathroom?", so you're not left trying to create an international body language signal for this particular question.

WHAT A NICE GESTURE!

Probably more than anything else, gestures are a source of amazement between cultures. It's as though people accept the differences in personal space requirements, and can even understand the touch/don't touch thing, but when it comes to using our hands to indicate what we mean, the common reaction from culture to culture is, "Do you know what that means?", because, of course, several cultures can affix a different meaning to one single gesture. It's the same exact gesture, only dirtier—or nicer, as the case may be.

Ooh, That's Bad!

Let's say you're visiting Argentina. You've taken the time to learn a little bit of the language (thank you very much), and you understand that Argentines need less personal space than you do. Why, you barely batted an eye (which, you'll remember from Chapter Three, is sometimes a sign of nervousness) when your waiter took you by the arm to seat you. Now he's come by to ask how your meal is and you smile and give him the "OK" sign. He, in turn, curls his lip in disgust and storms off. Your Argentine friends are shocked by your behavior and you're left feeling completely confused. Should you have indicated that the meal was horrible?

Well, in a sense, you did. Or you at least offended the waiter horribly. Had you done more research on the country, you would have found that the hand signal that Americans use to signify that everything is hunky-dory is actually an obscene gesture in many countries. Your friends at the table chastise you immensely for not knowing this. Well, great, you think. Nice of anyone to tell you before now.

Later, after the waiter has calmed himself down, he comes by to clear the dishes and to ask if everything was to your liking. You, of course, have a mouth filled with food. Surely it would be rude to answer with meat showing between your teeth, and you don't want to offend him any more than you already have. You offer him the brightest closed-mouth, genuine smile you can muster and give him the thumbs-up sign. Now he looks at you as though you're the Devil. Your friends are pretending they don't know you.

You see, you did it again. The thumbs-up sign is also considered offensive and vulgar in many countries.

You wouldn't want to use the OK sign in France, either— or at least not to gesture that everything is great. In that country, this hand signal means "zero."

Now, aren't people internationally minded enough to recognize an American gesture for what it is? Some are, and some aren't—but that isn't the point. If a foreigner came to this country and inadvertently flipped you the bird, how would you react? Possibly not with hostility, but certainly with confusion—because you may not be aware that pointing with the middle finger is commonplace in other countries. Just as you may not be up on international gestures, the locals in the countries you're visiting may not be, either, despite the proliferation of the American culture throughout the world. So . . . when in doubt, keep those hands to yourself.

Come Here!

So you've left Argentina (and they were glad to see you go) and you're off to China, where you'll be very careful not to use your gestures to signal how much you're enjoying the food and the culture.

While there, you'll be staying with a lovely family. They've welcomed you into their home, you're keeping your eye contact to a minimum, and things seem to be going great. You haven't given anyone the thumbs-up sign just yet, so you're feeling comfortable that you're not going to make any huge gesturing errors on the international scale. You're trying to raise yourself up from where you're seated and you find you're stuck. You just can't get up. You beckon for your hostess to help—you don't know the words, so you use your index finger, curling it in towards you to indicate that you need her.

If she helps you at all, it will be because she feels it's her duty. This method of calling someone toward you is used only for animals in China and is considered impolite. In most Asian countries, the proper way to motion someone to come to you is to point the hand down toward the floor and move the fingers together in a scratching movement.

Time to pack up? Perhaps.

It's Just a Friendly Little Game

Moving on, the next stop in your whirlwind tour of the world is Turkey. Again, you've taken the time to learn a little something about the culture. You know that you might be kissed on the cheek when someone says hello to you, and you will not, under any circumstances, point the sole of your foot to anyone, because you know this movement is very insulting to Turks. You've already caused enough trouble in two other countries with your gestures. You're toeing the line here.

While in the marketplace, a child wanders by. He's just so darn cute, you can't help but get down on his level to say hello. He's a little giggly thing, and you know just the way to amuse him: by playing "got your nose."

Suddenly, the child is swept away by his mother, and you're lambasted for your actions. What have you done now? You were only being friendly.

Well . . . unfortunately for you, when you put your thumb between your index and middle finger, you effectively flipped the kid off. This is the Turkish version of giving someone the finger.

So. That didn't go so well.

Bloody Hell

Having offended the citizens in three countries, you figure it's time to move on to the United Kingdom. After all, they're just like us, but with better accents, right? They'll get you, they'll welcome you, and there's nothing you can do to offend these people, you're quite sure. Why, you've even met some Brits during your lifetime, so you know exactly what you're getting yourself into.

You and a British friend go down to the local pub for some bangers and mash. You order two pints, but apparently, the bartender didn't hear you. He asks, "How many?"

Because he didn't hear you the first time, you figure he won't hear you the second time, and anyway, your voice is a bit hoarse from all the screaming you've done while running away from irate people all over the world. So you hold up two fingers, with your palm facing toward you . . .

And you find yourself out in the street. All right, you're thinking, how could signaling how many drinks you wanted possibly offend someone? Geez, it's just a number. True, but in the U.K., this is also the way of sending the same message we send with a single middle digit.

Time to go home? Yes, probably.

SEALING THE DEAL WITH BODY LANGUAGE

Of course, it's not good to offend regular citizens while you're visiting their homelands. It's also not wise to offend foreign colleagues, whether they're coming to your office or you're headed over to their turf. As we've already discussed throughout this book and in this chapter, small, seemingly innocuous gestures—or the absence of them—often make the subtle differences in our day-to-day dealings, whether they're business or personal relationships.

This section will give you an overview of what kind of business body language you might expect to find in various regions of the world. By knowing the body language of the culture you're working with, you're definitely going the extra mile to win their favor (while simultaneously ensuring that you're not inadvertently offending anyone).

Asian Business

Knowing that Asians are reserved and generally more soft-spoken than Americans is paramount to succeeding in this business sector. What should you absolutely know about body language before meeting with an Asian bigwig?

➔ Eye contact is kept to a minimum.

➔ Silence is not a sign of disapproval; it's very much a part of the culture.

➔ Business cards should be printed in English and the language of the respective country. In China, you should hand your card to another person using both hands. In Taiwan, you should put the card right into your pocket and read it later; doing so in front of the other person is considered rude.

➔ Avoid conflict and find creative ways to say no (such as "I'm not sure we're going to be able to do that.")

➔ Bowing is used as a greeting, though it's not always necessary these days, because the handshake has been incorporated into Asian dealings as well. (Your handshake should not have a killer grip, but should be rather light.) Still, it won't kill you to offer a slight bow as a sign of goodwill—and it will probably make a great impression.

How low should you bow? Bowing is all about reverence, so the person who is "lower" on life's scale bows lower (you would bow lower to your boss, for example, but anyone that you supervise would bow lower to you). The longer the bow is held, the more respect you're showing to the other person. If you're in doubt, bow slightly lower than the other person.

European Business

We tend to think that all Western cultures are the same. Not so. What do you need to know before planning your business trip to Europe?

→ A handshake is the standard form of greeting (and also is to be offered at the close of a meeting), and in many countries, it's appropriate to offer your hand to everyone, men and women alike. But in the U.K., for example, women should extend their hand to a man. Also in the U.K., the proper handshake has a light grip, but in Switzerland, the handshake is firm. Be aware that these discrepancies exist and do your research thoroughly before setting sail.

→ In France, it's rude to sit with your legs splayed. Don't do it.

→ Germans never shake hands or speak to one another with their hands in their pockets.

→ The thumbs-up sign is perfectly acceptable in Germany and France.

→ The "OK" signal is a rude gesture in Germany.

And in most European countries, showing up to a meeting is crucial. Don't be late.

Remember, the best way to make sure you're successful in sending the correct body language signals is to do thorough research on the world region you're headed to. Don't try to fake it.

the dating game

CHAPTER NINE: If you don't call it the dating game, then it's simply the Game. You know what it is—determining what kind of signals a stranger or a friend or coworker is really sending. Is he really flirting, or is it just wishful thinking (or arrogance) on your part? Certainly you can't be misreading all of the nonverbal communication coming your way—or are you? Many people do. Some women flirt without really meaning to, and some men try to flirt and fail miserably (and vice versa on the sexes). This chapter will give you a fair idea of how to determine whether someone is looking for love—or if he just has something in his eye.

JUST FOR KICKS

Flirting is either a fun little diversion for you or a serious headache if you just can't figure out the opposite sex. Take this quiz to see where you stand in your interpretation of flirting techniques. There's no shame in not getting the answers right—flirting is a confusing topic, which is why we're discussing it at great length here.

1. If a man looks your way several times, he's probably interested in you.

   a) True
   b) Not necessarily
   c) False

Answer: a. Men typically aren't masters of faking eye contact. If he's caught your eye several times, he's lookin'.

2. A woman's touch to a man's arm is a sure sign that she's looking for more than casual conversation.

   a) True
   b) False

Answer: b. Some women are big touchers—they touch everyone, all the time. A long, lingering touch is a better indication that she's interested.

3. A head tilt during conversation indicates that a woman is merely confused by what a man is saying.

   a) True
   b) False

Answer: b. The head tilt during the mating ritual indicates friendliness and is an attempt to convey innocence. It's a woman's way of saying she isn't going to hurt the man.

4. Leaning in toward a potential mate during conversation shows that you like what he or she is saying.

    a) True
    b) False

Answer: a. You're decreasing the amount of personal space between the two of you, which is your way of saying you'd like to hear more.

5. Angling away from a person of interest drives him wild.

    a) True
    b) False

Answer: b. Turning away from someone you'd like to get to know better only sends the message that you're not interested.

6. Eye contact between interested parties at opposite ends of the room should be held for fifteen seconds at a minimum.

    a) True
    b) False

Answer: b. Stare at her this long, and you're likely to scare her. Staring is a sign of aggression, which just doesn't fly with a lot of women.

7. A woman's shrug indicates that she's interested in a man.

    a) True
    b) False

Answer: a—probably. It depends on her other body language signals. Shrugging can be another way of showing her innocence and approachability (or a way of emphasizing bare shoulders), but it can also indicate uncertainty.

8. Keeping your hands in your pocket shows that you're relaxed and open to new situations and people.

    a) True
    b) False

Answer: b. Hiding the hands is usually considered to be a deceptive move. Put them out there and let them do the talking.

9. Eye level conversation is not important when you're flirting with someone.

    a) True
    b) False

Answer: a. Eye level conversation is not important at this stage. A man wants to feel dominant here—as long as the woman is comfortable in that knowledge, then it's OK to let him be on higher ground.

10. Knowing how to work your body language will ensure you countless dates.

a) True
b) False

Answer: It's anybody's guess. Your personality has as much to do with your success rate as the way you carry yourself.

Each of these concepts will be discussed in this chapter. There's a lot of ground to cover, so let's get started . . .

UPPER-BODY FLIRTING TECHNIQUES

Women have quite the arsenal with which to defeat men who may be resistant to their charms. In fact, men often walk away from professional-grade flirts wondering why they're feeling strange, especially if the man in question is a friend whom you've been trying to woo for some time. There comes a turning point in these relationships, where he finally notices your eyes or your lips, and then he's just a goner. The trick is getting him to look at you in this way.

Of course, there's also the bar scene, where women are faced with men they don't even know. It's actually somewhat easier to draw a man to you under these circumstances because he's probably looking for some attention—or at least is unlikely to be averse to it. The difference between being a subtle flirt and an obvious one can make all the difference in your success rate. Quality men aren't really often interested in women who've been around (sorry, but it's true).

So . . . how can you use your body language and your upper body to flirt—without making a spectacle of yourself and land a guy? Read on.

The Arms and Shoulders

We briefly discussed the use of the arms in Chapter Five. A feminine arm is a thing of beauty to men, and most of them don't even realize it. If you have a decent set of arms, don't be afraid to show them off. You don't have to parade around in halter tops, but a tank top or a sleeveless dress might be an option you're comfortable with (obviously, this is not an option for most work settings—we're talking about social situations here).

The feminine arm accentuates the differences between the sexes. A woman's arm is generally weaker-looking than a man's. This sends him the signal that you're harmless and that you need someone to protect you.

Use those arms subtly—drape one across the back of a chair. Reach out ever so slowly to pick up your drink. Put those arms to good use—in other words, don't cross them (even if it's the most comfortable position for you), and don't hide them.

Men are also drawn to bare shoulders. Use them to your advantage. Bare them and shrug them—not so much that it looks like you have a nervous twitch, but enough so that he'll take note of them. (The shrug is, among other things, a sign of compliance.) Don't forget to angle those shoulders towards the guy you're chatting up. Talking to him while seated on a bar stool facing forward (while he's seated to your side) does not send the message that you're interested in him. Don't be surprised when he gives up.

The Hands

Men also react to feminine hands, which doesn't mean that hands have to be perfectly manicured—just well kept. Again, hands accentuate the differences between the genders. Large, well-worn hands are thought to be masculine (and a leftover sign of the hard work that our ancestral hunters performed while taking care of their women), while smaller, well-groomed hands are more feminine (though there's no official word on how well groomed the hands of the female gatherers of yore were).

Use your hands. Let them do the talking. Reaching out to plant a light, lingering touch on a guy's arm while the two of you talk tells him that you're enjoying his company. Placing your hands where they can be seen is a sign of openness, not only on the dating scene, but also in society in general. Hidden hands are thought to be a sign of deception. So keep them out there—don't jam them in your pockets (a move that also affects your posture, which should be nice and straight) or hide them under the table. Let them loiter over papers (in the office) or over your glass (at a party).

The Head

The head-tilt is another sign of compliance, friendliness, and also a way to say, "Look how feminine I am," as men don't engage in head-tilting as much as women do. It's a nice tactic to employ, as long as you can make it look natural (just a slight tilt is sufficient—you needn't work to get your cheek all the way down to your shoulder) and you don't overuse it. (It can come off looking way too "cutesy.")

Along with the shoulder shrug, the head-tilt is a welcoming gesture, a way of telling your prospect that you're not going to bite (unless he says it's all right). Children often use both of these gestures, and carrying them over to the flirting scene makes you look innocent enough to approach.

And what about hair twirling? It depends on the context—if you were to sit in a meeting twirling your hair, for example, your boss would likely think that you weren't paying attention. Twirling the hair is generally thought to be a sign of flirting, though, in social situations. And again, this is something you should do only if you can make it look natural and not too childlike (as this is another move that's associated with small kids). Touching a man's hair, by the way, is usually a pretty bold, sudden move—it's moving right into his personal space. Even if it's done under the guise of determining what kind of conditioner he should be using, be aware that he might shy away from this kind of touching simply because you're on his turf now. More on how to effectively use personal space later in this chapter.

The Eyes

Successful flirting depends on knowing how to use eye contact to your advantage. You can have all the other moves down pat—but if you avoid looking him in the eye, you're just spinning your wheels. So make eye contact—and hold it for longer than is socially acceptable, but not so long that someone could say that you're staring. Look away for a short while, and then do it again. Make sure your eyes are open wide—again, this makes you look innocent. A side-long glance is also very useful. It's coy, and it's really only a technique that people use in flirting and spying on other people—which adds a little excitement to this Game.

A friendly little eyebrow flash goes a long way towards establishing rapport with a potential suitor. It opens up your face and eyes, which makes you look approachable. Knitting the eyebrows together or arching only one is akin to telling him he's done something you find less than attractive.

Batting the eyelashes is a common unintentional response to excitement—and an intentional flirting technique that makes women appear innocent and childlike. But wait, you say. Isn't batting the eyelashes a little too obvious? Not if you know how to do it correctly. The right way to bat the eyelashes is to blink two or three times and to do it so quickly that no one will look at you and ask, "Wow, what's wrong with your eyes?" The eyelash batting we see in movies and TV tend to be exaggerated, comedic examples—so don't use what you see in the media as a template for adding the eyelash-bat to your own flirting repertoire. Use your own mirror to perfect this move.

Winks are a move that indicate a secret between two people; they should be used in the flirting realm sparingly and only after they've been perfected with practice (so keep that mirror around). We talked briefly about winks in Chapter Three. The problem with winking is that it's so obvious a move that hardly anyone uses it anymore, or at least not in a serious way. Some people are very good at the subtle wink, and if you can pull off a wink that's just barely noticeable, then it might be a nice addition to your flirting regimen.

Equal Footing?

Eye level conversation is not as important during the flirting ritual as it is during other conversations—at least not from a woman's point of view. It's all right to stay seated when you're flirting with a man, as long as it's not putting an awkward distance between the two of you. (If he's seated on the edge of your desk and you're in your chair, you're OK. If he's standing on the opposite side of the conference table and you're sitting six feet from him, the tension is going to be lost.) Remember, eye level conversation is important to make both parties feel like equals in the conversation. The person standing will feel—and be perceived as—the dominant one.

When you're trying to snag a certain guy, you probably don't really care if he feels dominant (that will change later, of course). This is something else that underscores the differences in the sexes, where men are perceived to be strong and women need men to take care of them. Letting him feel a little dominant during this flirting song-and-dance routine might just allow him to realize how feminine you really are, which, after all, is what you're aiming for.

PULLING OUT THE BIG GUNS

No, that's not all. There's much more to a woman's body language and flirting. There's the way you physically move, the amount of personal space you're willing to sacrifice, and the vibe you put out, all of which can play a huge part in determining whether you'll be successful on any given evening.

Move It

No, you don't really have to walk with a washing-machine swivel to attract a guy. However, the theory (according to scientists) is that men are intrinsically attracted to young women who can bear their children. Most women inherently walk with a feminine sidle which slightly shows off the hips (supposedly the focal point of men, being that this is where those babies will be stashed for nine months) moving from side to side. If you know that your walk could use a little help (in other words, it's anything but feminine), start working on it. Make sure your toes aren't pointing in while you walk, but also make sure that they aren't pointing outward, in penguin fashion (according to some studies, this walk can intimidate men).

Dancing is a flirting ritual that you either love (if you can boogie like nobody's business) or hate (if you couldn't find your rhythm stashed in your pocket). Shakin' it is actually an ancient form of movement which has been studied—though not in depth—by anthropologists in an attempt to answer the question, why? Why do humans feel compelled to dance? What would make people want to get up out of their seats to move their feet, wave their arms, and gyrate? One theory is that dance is somehow related to someone's perception of themselves—for example, a confident person is much more likely to go out on the dance floor, claim his territory, and reaffirm his status as Mr. Something Special.

Another theory is that dancing simply makes people more visible to each other. We put our entire selves on display—the size, shape, and condition of our bodies, our state of mind, and how we choose to express ourselves. We're also freer to touch people when we dance, and likely to feel drawn toward other dancers (people who are similarly moved to express themselves through dance). So dancing not only allows us to show off what we've got, it also allows us to evaluate prospective partners.

You may be so drawn in by the music that you don't care what you look like when you dance. That's fine and well as an expressive way of living your life, but if you're using dancing as a means of flirting, practice in front of your mirror. Remember, you are making yourself more visible just by being on the dance floor. Get those moves down before you put on your little show.

Sharing the Air

In Chapter Six, we discussed humans' need for personal space. Successful flirting relies on the careful invasion of another's territory. We discussed cultural differences in Chapter Eight, noting that in some cultures, people stand very close to one another when they talk, and this is sometimes mistaken by foreigners as an invitation to something other than friendly rapport. In this country, we generally stand about two and a half to three feet apart when we talk to people we don't know. But let's say you want to get to know someone—a member of the opposite sex—better. How can you get closer without forcing him to back off (an unconscious move on his part that will only hurt your attempts)?

Try this: If you're standing, give him the minimum amount of space—about two to two and a half feet from you. Then angle yourself off to the side, still facing him, of course (your bodies forming somewhat of a V). Now you've just eliminated more space between the two of you—your shoulders are probably about a foot apart, but because you're on an angle, there's still the perception of each of you having plenty of space. In reality, you're inside his intimate space, and if you're working the rest of your body language correctly, he may just succumb to what he thinks are your charms.

Leaning in towards another person while talking is another way to eliminate some of that pesky personal space between the two of you. You'll be sending the message that you don't want to miss one word.

People are often forced inside each other's personal space in crowded settings, so you may not have to do any of the work. Now you'll concentrate on the accidental, lingering touch. Say the two of you will bump elbows. Don't pull away like you've burned your delicate arm on the stove. Give it a second or two before you pull away. You've just knocked personal space out of the ballpark, and you're rounding the corner toward home. Make sure your breath is fresh.

The Most Important Aspect of Flirting

What is it that draws most men to women? Is it the eyes, the hair, the hands, the way you walk? It's all of those things, of course—and one thing more. Your vibe. Do you seem like a fun, outgoing person? You don't have to be willing to put a lampshade on your head, but you should seem open enough to the idea of meeting new people and getting to know them. If you seem closed off, you're eliminating a lot of possibilities for yourself. Men are simply unlikely to approach a woman who looks intimidating or angry at the world.

How can you give off a warm vibe?

Smile. Insanely simply advice? Yes. But it's also completely necessary. It shows off your mouth, making it completely unnecessary for you to pout or purse those lips, two moves that can come off looking goofy if not done well.

Make eye contact with your prospects. Looking down at the floor makes you appear shy; staring straight ahead may give off an air of aloofness.

Use your angling effectively. Face the person you're interested in speaking with.

Don't cross your arms. Sure, it's comfortable, but in the flirting realm, it might make you look a bit uptight.

Don't jam your hands in your pockets. Ditto.

In short, use your body language to act friendly towards a guy you're interested in. It's the first step to drawing him into your little world.

ADVICE FOR MEN

Most men know that women shy away from guys who come on too strong, probably because women don't ever want to think that they're simply the latest conquest or that they could be just anyone (the inherent danger of excessive male flirting—women tend to think you put the moves on everyone). You never want a girl to think that if she turns you down, you'll just move on down the line to whomever is sitting next to her. Part of the flirting ritual is having to do a little work for the prize.

Key Move: Subtlety

In general, men don't employ little touches the way women do. Men who are "touchers" are often perceived as being on the make, or even a little creepy. Accidental brushes against a woman's arm or leg can be very subtle and incredibly effective for opening her eyes to the possibility of you.

Perfecting the art of eye contact is crucial for men who are interested in a girl seated across a crowded room. When her eyes meet yours, hold that eye contact for two or three seconds, being careful not to stare, which can come off as stalker-like. Look away, and then repeat the process. If she looks back at you, you're doing well. Read the rest of her body language (discussed in the previous sections of this chapter) to know if she's flirting back.

And what if you can't catch her eye? Assess her body language to evaluate whether she's approachable. Is she sitting with her arms folded over her chest, eyes straight ahead, and not looking like she's interested in engaging with the world? She's probably not interested in chit-chat. If she's smiling and looking all over the room, though, you can be fairly sure that she's a friendly sort. She won't toss a drink in your face, at the very least.

Reading Her Signals

The trouble that most men seem to have when it comes to flirting is reading the woman. Is she just friendly, or is she interested in something more? Though touching is certainly one way that women flirt with men, some women touch everyone, all the time, not realizing the effect it has on the opposite sex. You'd have to know a woman fairly well to evaluate whether her little touches are flirting or merely part of her friendly banter.

There are several ways to know if she's returning your vibes:

→ The amount of eye contact

→ Her use of personal space

→ Lingering touches

A woman who's interested will return your gaze—several times—and will use her eyes to flirt when she's speaking with you (read the earlier section on this topic). The majority of women simply don't widen the eyes, hold eye contact during a conversation, and bat their eyelashes for a man they'd rather not get to know.

If she initiates the reduction of personal space between the two of you—or if she's forced closer to you by crowded conditions but doesn't back away when she has the chance—there's a pretty good chance she's getting closer to you on purpose. It's just human nature to keep a healthy amount of space between ourselves and people we don't know—or don't plan to know—very well.

Lastly, the lingering touch can be a sign of her true intentions. Unlike the little pat on your arm or the nudge to your shoulder, a lingering touch is intentionally drawn out for the purpose of revving your engine. How can you tell the difference if you hardly know her? If her hand brushes yours at the table and she doesn't draw it away quickly, that's a lingering touch. If your legs knock together when you're seated next to each other and she doesn't change her position, that's a lingering touch. (There's a subtle difference between the friendly touch and this maneuver in her bag of tricks, and it can be very hard to tell the difference if she's a real pro at flirting.)

Review the flirting techniques that women use and practice your eye contact . . . and, of course, once you've read her body language, don't be afraid to make the first move.

liar, liar

CHAPTER TEN: It's something everyone wants to know: How to spot a liar. There are different degrees of lying. There's the little adjustment of the truth (the white lie), the avoidance of the issue (lies of omission), and the whopper (which bears little resemblance to fact). We like to think that we can spot a liar, or at the very least, know when those closest to us are being untruthful. The fact is that most people tell at least one fib every day without giving it a second thought. This chapter will give you some idea of what you're really looking for when you're searching for the truth.

DIFFERENT PEOPLE, DIFFERENT LIES

People lie. That's the bottom line. Some of us (this writer included) are very trusting, almost naïve, and figure that most people tell the truth most of the time. It just doesn't make sense to us that people would lie when telling the truth is usually easier and less painful in the long run (people who don't lie don't have to remember their stories, cover their tracks, and/or keep a running tally of whom they've told which lie to). In order to spot a lie, you have to be looking for it.

Do you have to become a cynical nonbeliever of everything anyone ever tells you in order to spot a liar? No. Some people definitely go that route, but for most people, having a healthy amount of skepticism—and a keen eye for observing behavioral patterns—is enough to see through a ruse or to protect yourself from a scheme.

It's also important to know when people lie: Children lie when they're faced with punishment. Friends and family members lie to save you from harsh reality. Spouses lie when they've been engaging in some secret activity, whether it's an affair or a three-month spending spree. Bosses lie when they want their employees' toil to benefit the company without fair compensation. Salesmen lie in order to get their hands on your money. Politicians lie ... well, because apparently, they're programmed to. (But mostly because they're protecting their images and jobs.)

Of course, because people are humans, these lines cross and blur with stunning regularity. Your friend might be lying to you because she's robbing you blind and dating your boyfriend behind your back (which are both secret activities, but also things she doesn't want you to know about: After all, you're pals, and she doesn't want to hurt your feelings).

Hmm. Maybe you do need to become cynical to spot a liar . . .

ALMOST A LIE

Along with the out-and-out lie, we have to consider the almost lie—the lie of omission or whatever someone tells you when they don't have the facts, and they know they don't have the facts.

The Elected Fibber

Consider this scenario: A key politician is speaking about the current romantic scandal he's involved in. For half an hour, he stands at his podium, reading a speech and using rehearsed hand, eye, and head gestures (ooh, the guy's good—it's hard to spot a lie when the other person has done everything they can to eliminate tell-tale body language signs). When the floor is opened up for questions, you'd better have your glasses on if you want to know the truth about what's really happening between him and his alleged mistress. This guy will likely give away few clues.

The first question is regarding his use of tax money to buy the lady a fur coat. The politician answers, using direct eye contact, "She was a destitute person, and she was cold. I purchased that coat using funds designated for helping the homeless." You notice that he has raised himself up on his toes as he says this, and you jot this down for your final analysis.

Question number two comes at him: Why is the woman living in his home? Surely there was room for her at the homeless shelter. The politician, raising his eyebrows, answers, "Actually, the shelter was full. My wife welcomed her into our home."

The third questioner wants to know if this woman has been arrested for extortion in the past. The politician licks his lips, tilts his head, frowns, and says, "I am not aware of any such record."

The last question is about the state of the politician's marriage. Will he be divorcing his wife? The politician purses his lips, frowns, and shakes his head. "No," he says, finally. "Definitely not."

So is this guy telling the truth? It would appear, from his body language, that he responded truthfully to the first two questions. Raising up on the toes is literally elevating oneself, something people do when they believe the words they're saying. Raising the eyebrows, as he did in responding to the second question, is another form of doing this same thing.

While eye contact is usually a good way to evaluate how truthful someone is being, many liars are quite skilled at faking and making an appropriate amount of eye contact. A politician is usually well rehearsed by his advisors as to how much eye contact he should maintain. We'll discuss the use of eye contact in lying later in this chapter.

It seems as though he's not so sure of his answers to the third and fourth questions, however. Licking his lips is a method of doing what's called the tongue-push (where the tongue is made visible briefly—this isn't a full circling of the lips), and is a good indicator of doubt in what one is saying. Pursing the lips, frowning, and shaking the head are also signs that someone may not be lying, exactly, but that they may not have all the pertinent information, either.

This is far different than a situation where someone honestly believes he's answering a question truthfully—in this case, we can probably say that this guy may have heard whisperings of his alleged girlfriend's prior arrests, but that he's never heard confirmation of those facts. And while he's not going to divorce his wife, that doesn't mean that his wife hasn't already handed him separation papers.

It's Not a Lie—It's Just Not the Truth

People try to get away with telling these lies of omission all the time. But you can tell when there's more than what you're being told—even if the "more" is just that the person doesn't really know what he's talking about.

What kind of body language indicates that someone is unsure of what they're saying?

Self-touches. These are self-comforting measures. Someone who rubs their own arm while they speak, for example, or touches their face or plays with their hair while speaking to you is probably feeling anxious and unconsciously soothing themselves in this manner.

Tense-mouth signs. Pursing the lips is a big clue that

someone is thinking about something. The lips drawn together in a tight line indicate real tension, a sign that this person knows that he's hiding something.

Tilting the head. Another movement people engage in when they're thinking . . . probably about how to scoot around certain, possibly damaging facts.

Looking down. It's this simple: People who aren't being completely honest don't want to look you in the eye—unless they're very good at this lying business, in which case, you should run in the opposite direction as soon as you learn the truth.

Shaking the head. Something most people do when they're unsure of something.

One hand to the back of the neck. Indicates confusion (discussed in Chapter Five).

Shrugging. Shows that someone is feeling helpless and not completely in control of the situation.

Many of these signals carry over into actual, deliberate lying, which we'll discuss in the next section. One big difference between lying and omitting the truth is that the person who is telling a lie of omission may not show a lot of signs of anxiety, because he's not exactly being untruthful. What he's telling you is at least partly true, so he may not feel the least little twinge of guilt, which is something that can often cause an actual liar to experience a physical reaction to the story he's telling. Is it easier to spot a liar than a half-truth-teller? Read on, and be the judge of that yourself.

DIGGING DEEPER

Before you can really tell if someone is a lying son of a gun, you have to know that person. You have to have a chance to observe him interacting with others, and you have to interact with him yourself. When you know which behaviors are normal and which aren't, then you can establish which behaviors might be signs that he's lying to your face. It would be wrong, for instance, to think that your ultranervous brother is lying to you when he's nervous all the time, in every situation, and with everyone he comes into contact with. He's just constantly on edge. Your accusing him of lying might push him right off that edge, so make sure you know what you're talking about before you confront him with the evidence of his own telling behavior of deception.

Sorry, Bro

Let's use the nervous brother to discuss typical behavioral clues that someone may be lying to us. Let's say your brother visited you last weekend, and after he left, you noticed that you were missing quite a bit of cash. You confront him with this the next time you're face-to-face, and he denies it. He's flushing, his eyes are wide open and focused on you, he's shaking his head, and he's rubbing the back of his neck. Is he lying to you?

Can't tell. These are all signs of general nervousness—which would be clear indicators of deception in this case if he weren't always on the verge of a panic attack. He is looking you squarely in the eye, which is actually a sign that he's telling the truth, and if his eyebrows are raised, this is also indicative of him believing his side of the story.

Someone's Pants Are Burning . . .

Well, your brother has been ruled out as a suspect, and he probably won't be speaking to you for a while after you accused him of stealing, so you've got some time on your hands to track down the real culprit. You casually mention to your roommate over breakfast that you're missing a big chunk of change, and he nods a lot while concentrating on his cereal, but never looks up at you or even responds verbally. You press the issue, and he finally returns your stare and refuses to break eye contact. Then he leaves the room, telling you that he has no idea what you're talking about.

You might want to think about getting yourself a safe—and keeping your valuables in it. Unless your roommate normally behaves in this manner—first completely avoiding a topic and then becoming overly aggressive about it—there's a pretty good chance that he actually does know what you're talking about. The fact that he left the room and then decided to deny his involvement bolsters your theory of his guilt. He didn't want to look you in the eye while he lied.

How to Spot a Lie

So . . . what are the tell-tale signs of lying?

Eye contact. Either a complete lack of eye contact, hard staring, or looking down toward the floor. A refusal to back down from eye contact may be a sign of deception in a skilled liar who thinks he can manipulate you into believing him. Blinking excessively is also a sign of being untruthful.

Facial flushing. An uncontrollable sign of anxiety—but also something that happens to some people with the least little provocation.

Sweaty palms. Also a sign of nervousness that's not under our control.

Angling away from the accuser. The person doesn't want to talk to you—but why?

Arm or leg cross. Does the other person suddenly decide to cross his arms after you've accused him? Does one leg suddenly pop over the other? He may be hiding something.

Very fast or very slow head movements. Someone who nods too quickly, as though he's listening (like the roommate in the above example), or shakes his head like it's moving in slow motion may be overly nervous for a reason.

Self-touching. Again, a self-comforting measure for increasing anxiety. Touches to the mouth are supposed to be a strong indication of deception, as though the liar is trying to stop the lie from coming out.

Inability to stand (or sit) still. More anxiety.

Throat clearing.

Stammering.

High-pitched voice.

Obviously, these last three items deal with verbal responses, but these are very important—and easy-to-hear—clues that indicate that someone may be lying.

You probably noticed that just about everything on this list could be the result of feeling nervous, and you may reason that someone may respond to being accused by becoming anxious. This is true, and that's why you need to have a good feel for a person before you can really tell whether they're lying.

For example, if your normally solid-as-a-rock coworker says he's taking a personal day at the end of the week in order to catch up on work, but he's rocking back and forth in his chair and flushing as he's discussing this, he might just be taking off for a long weekend instead. He's showing signs of nervousness about a topic that shouldn't be at all nerve-wracking. His spoken message and body language are clearly at odds.

PROTECTING YOURSELF

Aside from assuming that everyone is lying to you (which really isn't the best idea, anyway, unless you're naturally skeptical and you just can't help feeling this way), how can you guard yourself from being the victim of lies?

Be being vigilant, by acknowledging that people do lie, and by using a few well-placed body language moves to send the signal that you did not just fall off the turnip truck, so to speak.

You Know It, Now Use It

Let's say you have a friend who is going through a messy breakup. He's always been prone to telling tall tales, so it doesn't surprise you when he begins to tell you now that his almost-ex has a terrible temper, that she smacked him around daily, and that she's been in prison before for assaulting another ex-boyfriend.

You know this woman, and she just doesn't seem capable of such a thing. Still, you never know what people do behind closed doors, so you decide to observe your friend's behavior as he's telling the story. He's rubbing his cheek, he's angled away from you and looking out the window, and his finger is just brushing his lip. The guy's lying to you.

When he turns back to face you, what are you going to do? Offer him sympathy? Pretend you didn't hear him? Tell him that you suspect he's feeding you quite the false (and creative) story? You can let him know that you don't believe him by responding negatively with your body language.

What are the classic defensive gestures that show your confidence? A hard glare. Feet placed wide apart while you're standing up straight. A frown. The tense mouth. Angling away from the person. Crossed arms will also definitely work to your advantage here.

What do these body language signals say to someone whom you suspect is being less than truthful with you? That you're not believing him. You are definitely closed off to his argument and are also feeling hostile toward him. Will this make him admit his guilt? Who knows? But when a liar knows that you aren't buying his story, he's not likely to continue his embellishing. At the very least, you might stop the liar in his tracks before he can do any more damage.

Beware the Skilled Salesperson

Now, here's where you have to be really skilled at reading body language in order to protect yourself. Just knowing that salespeople are trained in effectively using their body language to close deals should be enough to keep you on your toes whenever you're dealing with a car salesman, the salesgirl in your favorite boutique, or a real estate agent. Their job is to get you to pay for something—this is how they make their money. You'd better believe that they have invested their time learning how to make their body language work its magic on you.

How on earth can you protect yourself against a pro? It's not easy, and that's why people get taken all the time. Dishonest salespeople who put a lot of effort into learning to manipulate body language for their gain are really just well-paid, highly skilled liars. And unfortunately, there are so many of them that they give honest businesspeople a bad name. You really have to be wary when dealing with anyone who's selling you anything.

These people aren't going to make it easy for you to spot their deceptive body language cues. Your real estate agent may very well offer a genuine-seeming smile (yep, those crow's feet are wrinkling up, and the corners of her mouth are curling up instead of moving laterally across her cheeks) while she tells you that the railroad track next to the house you're considering buying is going to be dismantled, even though she knows that it won't be. She's not going to put her hands in her pockets and look at her feet while she intentionally lies to you, nor will she blush, or even stammer. She's been doing this for far too long. She's good at it. To her, it's just part of the job.

Is there any easy way to spot a lying salesperson? Eye contact seems to be the one area where professional fibbers still slip up from time to time. Natural eye contact is simply hard to maintain when you're intentionally lying. Take note of whether the salesperson seems to need to look off in the distance while discussing major matters of business with you—and then follow up by doing your own research. That's truly the best way to make sure you don't get taken in a business situation.

Sociopaths

Every now and again, you'll run into a person who lies for no apparent reason. This person will lie to make herself look more important than she is, she'll lie to garner sympathy for something that never happened to her, she'll lie about what she had for dinner, who she's dating, what kind of shoes she bought (and how much she paid for them), and where she'll be vacationing over the summer.

For the sake of an example, let's pretend your college roommate is coming for a visit. She's been having a hard time lately. Her company downsized, she lost her job, and because she's so highly skilled, she's overqualified for every job she's applied for. Her mother is ill, and her sister ran off with a biker gang. She desperately needs some TLC, and you're just the one to offer it to her. And it certainly doesn't hurt that you live just steps from the ocean.

While she's staying with you, her boyfriend calls. He's going to pop in for a few days, too. Once he arrives, the two of them take off for the beach, which, luckily, is just outside your front door. You see them cavorting in the sand and the sun, and you notice that for someone who is supposedly down in the dumps (she's been wallowing at your kitchen table for the past two days), she's suddenly awfully happy.

The jig is up. You know you've been had. You don't need to call her mother (who you're sure is feeling fine) to confirm that your friend somehow got herself fired (probably related to her lying) and that no one else will hire her because she has a reputation for being dishonest. And the sister in the biker gang? She doesn't have a sister!

The worst part is how convincing her stories are. She is the most skilled liar of them all, and may even have some sort of diagnosable mental illness going on. You probably won't be able to break down her body language to tell when she's lying; since she lies all the time, she may even think that she's telling you the truth. The one way to determine whether this person is truly lying about something (because you'd figure that one or two things she tells you have to be true—it's just the law of averages) is to question her about it and then observe her body language. Pathological liars tend to get incredibly defensive if something they've stated as fact (but isn't) is called into question. You won't even have to look for subtle signs of defensiveness—she'll glare at you, jab her finger in your face, and defend herself to the death.

So what do you do with this person? Let her get away with it? Nah. Show her your own body language as you hold open the door and boot her out. (No way she'll get the wrong message from that move.)

index

Angling, 85–87, 125, 135, 136
Appearance (grooming), 25–27, 28, 30
Arm gestures, 10, 13, 64, 68–70, 128–29, 136
Art, of body language, 7
Asian business, 120–21
Blushing, 60–61
Body types, 19–22
Child body language, 61–62, 107, 141
Chin, 58–59
Dancing, 133–34
Darwin, Charles, 2, 4
Dating, 123–39
    advice for men, 137–39
    dancing and, 133–34
    flirting priorities, 136–37
    flirting techniques quiz, 124–27
    hand holding, 100–102
    kissing, 103
    personal space and, 134–36, 139
    relationship body language I.Q. test, 103–6
    touching and, 135–36, 137, 138, 139
    upper-body flirting techniques, 127–33
Drumming, 25, 31
European business, 122
Eyebrows, 10, 11, 12, 14, 46, 131
Eye contact, 37–44, 46
    first impressions and, 24–25, 29, 30, 32
    flirting/dating and, 11, 14, 124, 125, 130–33, 136, 137–39
    lying and, 62, 145, 147
Eye(s), 33–46
    aggravating movements, 42–44
    angry, 45–46
    blinks, 40–41, 45

    glares/stares, 38–39
    level, 34–37, 105, 126, 132–33
    winks, 39–40, 132
Facial language, 30, 47–62
    blank expressions, 11, 14, 49–50
    blushing, 60–61
    of children, 61–62
    chin and, 58–59
    face shape and, 48–49
    jaw expressions, 56–58
    mouth/lip expression, 51–56, 62, 144–45
    nose and, 51
    smiles, 10, 12, 30, 55–56, 114, 136
    yawning, 59–60
Finger gestures, 32, 74–77
First impressions/perceptions, 15–32. See also Eye contact
    appearance (grooming), 25–27, 28, 30
    body types/judgments, 19–22
    handshakes, 16–19, 30, 31
    image, 22–27
    interviews, 27–32
    posture, 22–24, 30
Flirting. See Dating
Flushing, 11, 13, 146, 148
Gender-based judgments, 21–22
Gestures, 63–79. See also specific body parts
    cultural differences, 115–20
    nervous habits, 12, 66–67, 78–79, 146
    quiz, 64–67
Hand gestures, 10, 11–12, 14, 19, 25, 31, 65, 71–75, 114, 126, 129, 137, 145
Handshakes, 16–19, 30, 31
Head gestures, 67–68, 124–25, 129–30, 145
History, of body language, 2–3
Hugs, 96–97

Image, 22–27
Interviews, 27–32
Jaw expressions, 56–58
Judgments, 19–22
Leaning forward, 29, 31, 32, 84–85, 135
Learned body language, 3
Learning body language, 7–9
Lips/mouth, 51–56, 62, 144–45
Lying, 8, 140–53
  almost lies, 142–45
  children, 62, 141
  identifying, 146–49
  politician example, 142–44
  protecting yourself from, 149–53
  salespeople, 141, 151–52
  signs of, 8, 62, 66, 142–49
  sociopaths, 152–53
  voice cues, 62
Makeup, 11, 13
Natural (inborn) body language, 3
Nervousness, 12, 18, 66–67, 78–79, 146
Nose, 51
Palms-down gestures, 19, 72–73
Palms-up gestures, 11, 14, 19, 25, 65, 73
Personal space, 88–91, 111–12, 134–36, 139
Posture, 80–93
  angles, 85–87, 125, 135, 136
  defensive, 83–84
  first impressions, 22–24, 30
  interviews, 29, 30
  openness, 84–85
  personal space and, 88–91, 111–12, 134–36, 139
  power positions, 91–93
  standing/walking tall, 22–24, 81–83, 87–88
Power positions, 91–93
Relationship body language I.Q. test, 103–6
Respect, 109–11

Self-touching, 10, 13, 62, 66, 77–78, 144, 148
Sets of body language, 3
Shrugging, 126, 145
Signals, defined, 3
Smiles, 10, 12, 30, 55–56, 114, 136
Tests/quizzes
  flirting techniques quiz, 124–27
  gestures quiz, 64–67
  reading body language test, 9–14
  relationship body language I.Q. test, 103–6
Touch, 94–107
  cultural differences, 113–14
  flirting with, 124, 135–36, 137, 138, 139
  hand holding, 100–102
  hugs, 96–97
  kisses, 103
  obvious cues, 98
  power of, 95–96, 97
  relationship body language I.Q. test, 103–6
  self-touch, 10, 13, 62, 66, 77–78, 144, 148
  subtle cues, 98–100
Universal signs. See Worldwide body language
Verbal language, body language and, 4–6, 62, 148–49
Walking, 23–24, 87–88
Worldwide body language, 108–22
  Asian business, 120–21
  European business, 122
  gestures, 115–20
  personal space, 111–12
  respect, 109–11
  touching, 113–14
  universal signs, 114–15
Yawning, 59–60